About J

'Jacky Newcomb's books h
name in the study of angels and afterlife communication. Jacky's work is essential reading for anyone interested in learning more about this fascinating subject ...'

Uri Geller, www.urigeller.com

'A gift for all who believe and even more so for those who aren't quite sure! A treasure box of stories that will lift you up and brush your soul with angels' wings.'

Darcie D. Sims, PhD, CHT, CT, GMS, Director,
American Grief Academy, Grief, Inc.

About *An Angel Treasury:*

'Jacky Newcomb has compiled probably the most fascinating book on angels yet made available to the public.'

Colin Fry, star of *6ixth Sense with Colin Fry*

About *An Angel Saved My Life:*

'A beautiful read that will inspire and touch all who read it and bring them to the realization we are always surrounded by angels.'

Tony Stockwell, star of *Psychic Detective*

About *A Little Angel Love:*

'A little ray of sunshine that fits into your pocket! An uplifting and inspiring read when you need it most.'

David Wells, *Most Haunted*

About *An Angel by My Side:*

'Want reassurance you can trust? Then look no further than Jacky Newcomb, a well-known and highly respected name in psychic circles. Jacky's a brilliant storyteller – and down to earth with a great sense of humour … This book is … a compulsive read for anyone interested in the afterlife.'

Mary Bryce, editor of *Chat – It's Fate* magazine

An Angel held my hand

An Angel held my hand

Inspiring true stories
of the Afterlife

Jacky Newcomb
'THE ANGEL LADY'

HARPER element

HarperElement
An Imprint of HarperCollins*Publishers*
77–85 Fulham Palace Road
Hammersmith, London W6 8JB

The website address is: www.thorsonselement.com

This edition published 2010 for Index Books Ltd

First published by HarperElement 2007

1

A catalogue record of this book is
available from the British Library

ISBN 978-0-00-785776-0

Printed and bound in Great Britain by
Clays Ltd, St Ives plc

To

my loving family,

John, Georgina and Charlotte.

May angels always hold their hands.

And to

all my lovely readers.

Angel Light

Angel Light, Star Bright,
Whisper words of love.
Feel, sense, listen close
Hugs, caring arms.

Angel Wings, Special Things
Always staying close.
Touch, see, shining white
Safely by your side.

Jacky Newcomb

Contents

Acknowledgements

Once again, thank you to everyone who has contributed to the amazing stories in the book. Without you there would be no book.

Introduction

If you can imagine it, you can achieve it.
If you can dream it, you can become it.

William Arthur Ward

Wow, what a rollercoaster ride I have been on over the last few years. From depressed mother and housewife to bestselling author, interviewed many times by the national media. How did this happen?

If you are a regular reader of my work you will know that I consider myself just a normal mum – but a normal mum who has experienced a wide range of paranormal phenomena in her life. I have thoroughly enjoyed writing about my own experiences and collecting these stories for you and I am thrilled that you seem to enjoy reading them as much as I have enjoyed writing about them. Angels have certainly changed my life and I really love hearing how they have changed your lives too.

I believe we all have psychic experiences from time to time. You know when you just *know* who is at the door when you hear the bell ring, or you pick up the phone already knowing who is on the end of the line, or you think of someone you haven't seen for years and then bump into them the very next day. These things just happen a little more often to some of us!

I've had out-of-body experiences, had relatives visit in dreams with lifesaving messages, heard voices giving warnings whilst I've been driving in the car and enjoyed the sweet sound of a celestial choir. Once, when I was at the lowest point of my life, I remember having a chat with 'him upstairs'. 'God,' I said, 'I no longer have a clue what to do, so I'm leaving it in your hands.'

I honestly didn't care what happened next in my life. But within moments I found myself being lifted out of my body. I felt totally at one with the energy of the 'all that is'. No words can even begin to describe that feeling. It was the most intense love I have ever felt in my life. I was being held in the very 'arms' of God and filled with the most perfect peace, an unconditional love far stronger than anything a mother could give to her child. I believe that this is the love we go back to when we die and return to our life in the heavenly realms.

I never wanted to come back to my body again and would have done pretty much *anything* to stay in those loving arms. But suddenly thoughts of my husband and two children flooded into my mind and this immediately broke the 'trance' and I came back into my body.

My experience was temporary. It was just a top-up of love. I had to come back to carry on with my life and sort out my problems – with the help of angels, of course. But now I knew that ultimately everything was going to be OK. And you know what? Everything did work out in the end.

Why have these things happened to me? Why do they happen to anyone? They inspired me to start studying psychic phenomena – well, wouldn't you? I was desperately searching for explanations for my own experiences. Along the way I discovered that thousands and thousands of people all over the world had been through many of the same things that I had. I began collecting their stories and I want to share some of them with you here. Loving messages from the other side of life, angels who appear just in the nick of time, signs from pets to show they have made it safely to heaven, messages sent to children by deceased relatives – many stories are very dramatic and leave you almost breathless with wonder. Some are subtler, of course, but all are mini-miracles of life.

In most cases, angels of one sort or another are involved. In all of them, the experiences are amazing and defy explanation. One day we *will* understand how and why such things happen, but for now let's just enjoy these stories for what they are – wonderful and life-changing experiences that show that anyone's life can be touched by an angel. Miracles know no bounds.

Let me begin by sharing a little more of my own journey. Am I crazy? Perhaps – but come and enjoy the ride just the same!

An Angel held my hand

CHAPTER 1

Angels and Me

It is not your aptitude but your attitude
that determines your altitude.

Zig Ziglar

Like most children I was frightened of ghosts. I have an early memory of running across our landing screaming. I was six years old and we were living in a 100-year-old three-storey house in Birmingham. It was dark and I'd stepped out of bed to visit the bathroom, just a short sprint across the squeaky floor and out of the door to the left. As I walked through the open door, though, a strange white shape drifted in front of me and seemed to float in front of my eyes for a moment before disappearing at the other end of the landing.

For the briefest moment I wondered if my sister Debbie was playing a trick on me, but she was only six and was snoring loudly in the room behind me, along with my youngest sister Madeline. And the shape hadn't had any feet and had been floating a foot off the ground.

No, I guess she hadn't learned to levitate just yet! So what was it?

Terrified, I ran back into my room. Actually, this wasn't my usual room. I had my own bedroom, but once a year I was chucked out of it so an elderly aunt could come and stay. When she arrived, I was despatched to the 'big bedroom' that my two sisters shared. This old house had large rooms compared to modern homes and the three of us fitted easily into the space.

The aunt, Aunty Edie, was tiny. I remember she used to repeat everything she said at least twice and follow me and my sisters around, walking so closely behind us that when we turned round quickly she would bump into us. We found her slightly scary. It wasn't her fault, you understand. When you're aged four, six and seven, a woman in her late seventies is ancient! Aunty seemed so old to me then that I worried she might die in my bed. Would she come back and haunt me? Perhaps my floating vision was the result of my sleepless nights of worry rather than an actual ghost? I've never been too sure.

The house we were in at the time was no ordinary house. It had a lot of character to it, and that character included lots of scary bits. The walls held memories – some good and some bad – and anyone a little sensitive would find it easy to pick up on the energies of that spooky old property. I've always had a healthy respect for the supernatural and I'm sure growing up in such an eerie house sparked my interest from an early age, though I do look back on it with affection.

In many ways it was a fascinating place to live in. It had two large cellars and a wine store beneath the ground floor. The basement area was always freezing cold and we girls were never allowed down there on our own. The stone steps and hard concrete flooring made these rooms a great danger to small children. They were always kept locked with a large old-fashioned key that my mother used to hide. My sisters and I used to make up horrible stories to scare each other and other children, and if someone left the key in the door we would sometimes lock one another in, which always resulted in much frightened screaming as well as hysterical laughter. Kids can be horrible to each other, can't they?

The breakfast room had a collection of original servant bells hanging high upon the walls. Originally, Mum explained, they were wired up all over the house and the wealthy owners of yesteryear could summon their household servants from any room in the house.

The kitchen was more of an old-fashioned scullery. Stone steps led down to an old conservatory, which was always full of spindly geraniums, tomatoes and a great many spiders. My mum hated spiders and for many years we were all terrified of them too.

I remember we once found a locked tin in the conservatory cupboard that had been left by the previous owners. It remained locked for many years until, bored one day, we persuaded our kindly father to break into it. For years that tin had been full of imaginary treasures, but the reality was a little less exciting: tennis balls, golf balls and other balls of all shapes and sizes. This was hardly the treasure we had hoped for, but it kept three bored little girls quiet for a few hours at least.

I remember one day getting into a lot of trouble. One of my sisters and I had climbed onto the conservatory roof using the tree at the end to reach up. The thin panes of ancient glass could have shattered at any moment, but that thought never entered our minds as we crawled along the precarious glass until our mother spotted us and gave us a well-deserved telling-off.

We also used to slide all the way down the beautiful curved banister rails that ran right from the top of the three-storey house down to the bottom. We never had any thought of falling. How my poor mother managed to keep her sanity I shall never know.

The gardens of all the houses in the area were very long and narrow. Mum grew a lot of plants in ours and it made a wonderful place for imaginative games. We used to pick the flowers and eat the blackberries that grew along the lane that joined all the gardens together at the end. One day we discovered that maggots were living inside the blackberries and were all very sick – probably more from the shock of seeing the maggots than from eating them!

At the end of this lane there lived a little girl and her younger brother. As the oldest child in our family, I was allowed to visit her and play. Then one day I wasn't allowed to go anymore and Mum explained that the little girl's brother had died and the family was too sad to have visitors. It was a natural death; the little boy had had a hole in his heart. I'd never known a young person who'd died before and this was the first time I'd considered my own mortality. At the time I was already suffering from horrendous nightmares and I'm sure this experience didn't help.

Later on, while we were still living in this house, my dad suffered a horrific car crash. I remember waking up to the sound of the doorbell and creeping to the top of the stairs to see what was going on. Two police officers were at the door and I could hear them telling my young mother that her husband was in a serious condition.

Dad survived that crash, but nearly lost his life many more times over the following years, and my fears of dying were much exaggerated by these experiences in my young life. I was so terrified that my father might die that I dared not love him too much just in case. But of course you can't stop loving someone! I wish I had realized then that he would actually live through the car accidents, perforated ulcer, stroke, brain tumour, coma and many other things that happened to him through the years. These experiences were all very difficult, but perhaps they were part of his chosen life path? They certainly taught us, and Dad himself, many lessons about love. I remember saying to him one day, 'Thanks for teaching us about unconditional love, Dad.' 'That's OK, my darling,' he said, as if on some level he too understood.

Dad eventually changed his job and we moved to a modern family home in a new area. Not that it was safe, especially the way we three young girls carried on. One of my sisters would hang upside down from the top bar of the swing set and we would all climb trees. I even remember following my mother across a very busy main road as she rushed over to the corner shop on one day. Boy, was she mad at that! But children seem to manage to scrape themselves out of serious situations every single day. And perhaps our guardian angels were working hard even then?

Since that time many unexplainable things have happened in my life. Many of my family had these experiences, too, but I don't think we are special in any way and I've since discovered that lots of families have their paranormal 'secrets'! It's funny, some families talk about their paranormal experiences and other families keep them quiet, but if you open up the topic of conversation with a group of people, you soon discover that *all* families have 'unexplainable' experiences or people who have 'dabbled' with alternative healing or paranormal ideas of one sort or another. I have the most fascinating conversations about this with people at my local gym. It's amazing what you can talk about to strangers when sitting in a hot tub!

Some of our family stories have been passed down through the generations. They include premonitions, out-of-body experiences, lifesaving dreams, alternative and spiritual healing, 'invisible friends', mediumship (sending and receiving messages from the spirits of our loved ones on the 'other side' of life) and psychic abilities. As I said, I know my family is not alone in this. Research has shown these phenomena occur all over the world, to people young and old, of all religions and none, and all walks of life. Who knows, perhaps it's *normal* for families to have psychic experiences from time to time. Why not interview your own family members and see what you discover? It could be very revealing!

The scariest experience in our family was that of my grandmother, who regularly dreamt that her young son would drown, and he did. I also discovered that a great uncle, desperate for help for his daughter, who was deteriorating with multiple sclerosis, tried all sorts of 'alternative' healing techniques. My mother tells me that back then, in the 1960s, there were many people trying things like spiritual healing or the laying-on of hands. But not many like my uncle – a pillar of society, a clerk for the local town council! Great Uncle Ernie wore suits to work, not flowers in his hair, but along with his wife Mary he was prepared to try anything to ease the suffering of his daughter Jennifer. Healers were dispatched from Devon to Oxfordshire, where the family lived, and we heard that for days after the healing had taken place Jennifer was a lot better.

Another uncle, Eric, my dad's brother, also joined in with the healing sessions and he and Great Uncle Ernie would also try things like acupuncture and the wearing of copper bracelets to ease Uncle Eric's arthritis. This was at a time when these things were still 'alternative', although nowadays these treatments are easier to come across and you're not thought of as quite so weird if you use them.

I also found that other relatives were interested in ancient sites, paganism and magic. It's amazing what you can find in your own family if you delve deep enough.

Nowadays, because I am very open to these things, people will share their experiences with me, but often still in whispered tones. 'My great grandmother was a medium,' they will say quietly, or 'As a boy I would watch as the family attended séances to call up the dead ...' These events were always wrapped in secrecy! But I'll bet your family and friends will have amazing stories to tell if you ask them.

When I first started writing about paranormal experiences, my close family was worried about what others might think about me. Later we were all surprised to discover how many friends and other family members had already bought my books, often without realizing I had written them! On the other hand, one lovely man knew of me first as an author and later discovered we were distant cousins.

Magic exists in all of our lives and it's time we *all* stepped out of the magical cupboard and shared our amazing stories with each other. Fascinating stories of angel intervention are worth so much more when shared. I believe that the intention of God 'himself' is that we share 'his' miracles with the world. One person's positive paranormal experience reaches out and helps so many others.

Just as an example, one of my own daughters, like me, has experienced premonitions. We've even had very similar dreams on the same night. And my husband and I once shared exactly the same dream. In it we were together and felt as if we were detached from our bodies and having an out-of-body experience. Perhaps we were. Has this ever happened to you?

Throughout all of my books I've also talked about my own amazing and often bizarre experiences of afterlife contact. My dear Uncle Eric has often been in contact since his passing. The whole family has received communication of one sort or another from him. He appears in dreams and helps to create 'coincidences' when we need his help. He also loves to flash the lights, set off the smoke alarm and ring the doorbell – just to show us he's around and to have a little fun with us! At the moment, however, his wife is ill in hospital and he has withdrawn slightly from us so that he can spend time with her (in his capacity as a spirit of course).

In the meantime my father-in-law, Jack, who died nearly 20 years ago, has stepped in to take his place. However, he has 'technical difficulties' in reaching either me or my husband in dream visitation experiences. Apparently I sleep 'on a different level' and that's why he has difficulty in bringing me messages, while his son, my husband, blocks everything out when his head hits the pillow and never remembers *any* dreams. Fortunately, for some reason known only to the heavenly realms, my father-in-law *is* able to communicate with my sister Debbie when she sleeps and he regularly passes messages to us via her.

Loved ones often reach out from the 'other side' in dreams and visions in this way. These 'visits' are different from ordinary dreams in that we are very 'lucid' and aware during them. We know that the person appearing in the dream is dead and will often tell them so. But of course their spirit lives on and they are back visiting us.

These deceased loved ones watch over us and keep in touch with what is going on in our lives. They're not *real* angels in the traditional sense of the word, but they do act as our guardian angels on occasion. There are examples of them saving lives later on in the book.

I experienced this myself when a dream visitation saved my father's life. Briefly, my uncle appeared to me in a dream to warn me that my dad shouldn't have 'the operation'. We were all on holiday at the time and Dad hadn't even been taken ill at that point, so we were more than a little confused. The following day, though, he was rushed into hospital – in a foreign country. An operation was offered, but we refused it and flew him home, preferring to take him to our local hospital where his medical history was known. A simple procedure then saved his life. Would he have died if he'd had the operation abroad? We'll never know for sure, but I know what I believe.

Actually, I haven't always believed in help from the other side – or the other side itself. In fact I wasn't born with any belief at all really! 'I don't believe in God, Jesus or angels!' I announced to my startled religious education teacher at school. The poor man was so worried that he called my parents into school to discuss it. My mum wanted him to challenge me and make me put my point of view in class, but the poor teacher didn't really know what to do with this non-believer!

Like many people, I just thought the idea of a higher power seemed almost too good to be true. And if there was one, why were things the way they were? 'If there is a God why do bad things happen in the world?' I would ask. In fact I still do. If Jesus came to save us then why have we still not been saved?

I was very confident in my disbelief as a child and had conveniently forgotten some of the many paranormal experiences in my own short life. Had angels been there the whole time and I just hadn't noticed? In fact God had chosen to give me my proof – over and over again – and I had quite simply missed it. But I'm not the only one. How many people do the same? And how much proof is proof?

If only I had known then what I know now! Imagine how amazed I would have been to discover that in the future I would gather stories of lifesaving and life-changing encounters with guardian angels.

So many people have amazing experiences that they have never shared with anyone before. They often begin their stories with the phrase 'I've never told anyone this before but …' Fear of ridicule or disbelief is a good reason for people to keep quiet. I understand that. But angels can help us so much in life and it's good for us to know it! I am always amazed by how much our angels can do for us. No matter how many angel experiences I read, I am always stunned by their power. The fantastic real-life experiences I have been privileged to read bring me great joy – and I hope you feel the same.

Angels really do change lives and save lives. How can we recognize them? Their interaction with us is often subtle but sometimes dramatic. Not everyone is going to meet a 12-foot being in a golden light, but it does still happen on occasion. Mostly, though, angels appear just in time to sort out emergencies before disappearing into the night. They bring message of hope when all seems lost. They appear in dreams and visions and everyday life. Who knows, they might be the stranger at the bus stop or even merge briefly with your pet cat. Angels are everywhere and you could well have met one without even knowing it. Remember the saying 'Be not forgetful to entertain strangers, for thereby some have entertained angels unawares.'

I'll give you a little clue, though. Angels often appear with the lightest of blonde hair and piercing blue eyes, even if they are dressed as humans! You might want to watch out for that. Their clothing can also be a dead giveaway. They don't seem to understand fashion at all and often wear what we would consider inappropriate clothing for the time of year or the era. There is usually something that doesn't look quite right!

So many people have written to tell me about their own lifesaving experiences with both their human 'family' of 'angels' and the winged variety. Angelic contact really is going on all around us. Children, too, have amazing stories to tell of their own contact with loved ones who have died and their own foresights into the future and insights into the past. There is so much magic in our lives and so many of us are guilty of walking around with blinkers on. We miss things that are right in front of our nose.

I want to open your eyes to the wonders that are all around you. So many children want to be like Harry Potter and perform magic. So many of us want to live in a world where miracles exist. But what if I told you that we already can and they already do?

I know that you'll enjoy the angelic wisdom, messages and amazing lifesaving adventures in this book. By the end you're sure to be a believer!

CHAPTER 2

Angels in the Car

For he shall give his angels charge over thee
to keep thee in all thy ways.

Psalm 91:11

On a French motorway one day a car leaped the central reservation and hit a car on the other side of the road – head on. That car flipped over and over on the motorway, tossing the passengers around like clothes in a dryer. The box of wine that they had picked up at the airport flew up into the air and loose bottles started smashing around them. Open bags of food and make-up from the handbag on the floor of the back seat deposited their contents all over the car and then later, when it came to a halt, lay along the length of the carriageway as the car began to collapse like an empty cardboard box.

My sister Debbie had been in the back seat of that car. Sitting next to her had been her husband of two years and in the driving seat and front passenger seat had been their friends, a husband and wife. They had been on their way to visit another English couple who had made their home in France. It wasn't the first time they had visited them, but this time it turned out to be a very different journey.

My sister told me later about how she felt as the car rolled over. She said, 'I knew I was being protected. I knew I would survive, but I wasn't sure if my friends would make it.'

The car landed on its roof. Inside, everyone was hanging upside down by their seatbelts.

In the front one of my sister's friends said, 'Is everyone OK?' The silence, she said afterwards, seemed to go on and on. The other passengers were too deeply shocked to reply. *Were* they OK?

'Yes,' someone said eventually, and then another, then another …

Cars were driving past the accident and it was important to get out of the car as quickly as possible. People can do extraordinary things in times of danger. Strength appears from nowhere. Someone kicked in a window and the seatbelts were unlocked, resulting in the inevitable: everyone landing on their heads. Unbelievably, all four of them walked away from the crash with little more than cuts and bruises.

The woman who had hit them in her car was also fine, as were her young children, who had been in the car with her. Language difficulties then caused problems, but after several hours, still in shock, the group continued their journey. Eventually they arrived safely at their destination and fell into the waiting arms of their friends.

A type of calm had surrounded Debbie as the accident happened. 'No one screamed,' she said, 'no one yelled.'

I remember receiving a photograph on my mobile phone just minutes after the crash – she had taken a photograph of the accident and mailed it over – and then hearing her voice saying, 'I've been in a serious accident, but I'm OK. I just wanted to speak to someone. In fact we're all OK …'

Not wanting to worry anyone by ringing in the early hours of the morning, I left it until first light before I informed the rest of the family. 'They're all OK,' I reassured everyone, and each of us took it in turns to telephone Debbie and see how the group was doing. When losing your life seems so close, all you want to do is be with those you love, and failing that, a telephone call is the closest thing to hand. The more you can talk about it, the better.

Later the following afternoon I contacted a close family friend and explained what had happened. 'I know …' she said simply.

Rather bizarrely, her daughter had dreamed the whole thing. In the dream she had been a passenger in a car with her mother and they had driven past the mangled wreck of a car on the motorway. Her mother had told her, 'Don't look, because it's either Aunty Jacky or Aunty Debbie!'

At the time my sister and I looked very alike. She has naturally blonde hair and I'd recently lightened mine. Even people who knew us both very well had been muddling us up since my change of hair colour. Could this young girl really have seen the accident as it happened – probably at the exact moment – in her dream? I believe she did.

That wasn't the only paranormal experience relating to this story. Many months later my sister began having the dream visitations from my father-in-law Jack that I have already mentioned. He started to accompany her in the car as well. Driving along one day, she heard his voice clairvoyantly as he communicated with her from the other side of life. He called himself her 'driving angel' and she asked him, 'Were you with us the day of the accident?' He told her that he was and that he had surrounded the car with a white light of protection. This protection was what my sister had felt in the car, along with the knowledge that she was going to be OK. When she asked Jack why he had told her about it, he answered, 'Because I can!'

I've heard Jack myself when I've been driving. I swear it was his voice I heard one day telling me to pull over as I drove my four-wheel drive up to a narrow bridge. Moments later a white van clipped my wing mirror and I knew for sure that had I been just a little bit further over towards the middle of the road I would have been involved in a head-on collision. Jack's urgent voice saved me from an accident that day and potentially a serious injury. He was my angel that day!

This experience is typical of the stories that people share with me. A large percentage of these relate to people feeling that their lives have been saved by angels – both the winged variety and our loved ones on the other side of life – and so often this happens when they are in the car.

Our cars are so important to us. They get us to where we need to go. They give us the freedom to explore our world and be with the people we love, but they can also be very dangerous. In the wrong hands, or when conditions dictate, they can become lethal weapons. Maybe that's why so many angels sit with us when we drive?

Another reason for 'car angel' stories being so very numerous is that when we drive our mind is relaxed and therefore more able to receive messages from our angels. That meditative state that we sometimes get into when we are driving a familiar route is the perfect opportunity for our angels to reach in and communicate with us. That contact is very likely to be when our angels are providing us with inspiration or suggestions for life problems, but it can also involve them saving our very lives. Part of our angels' job is to protect us from harm. Your angels are certainly with you when you drive, as these stories illustrate.

A Mystery Voice

Lara Wells is from the UK. She is the editor and owner of the publication *The Psychic Voice*, so it's clear that she *knows* for sure that there is more to life than what we can see, feel and hear! Here is Lara's terrifying story:

On 14 February, our tenth wedding anniversary, my husband and I were travelling to view a house. Following an accident five months earlier my car had been replaced with an exact duplicate, a silver Vauxhall Tigra. My nerves had been frayed by the accident, but my spirit was willing to continue to travel by road. On this particular journey I was a passenger in the front and my husband was driving. My daughter Tabitha was in her baby seat in the back, behind my husband. She was 25 months old.

Driving conditions were cold and crispy but not icy and as we were driving along the road to find the house we wanted to view, my husband spotted some miniature ponies in a field to our left. Tabitha was getting bored, so my husband called out to her to point them out. I turned round to look at her and saw she had started to get agitated for no apparent reason. I turned my head back round to the windscreen and as I did so the front left-hand wheel hit a patch of mud. The car immediately veered off to the left, got sucked into the grass and was flung back out again onto the road. My husband was braking furiously and I could see a burgundy-coloured estate car to our right, so I just grabbed the steering wheel with my right hand and pulled as hard as I could to balance the out-of-control car. I was successful, but then a female voice said to me, 'Get the baby *now*!'

In a panic I turned to look and realized we were now heading straight for a tree. The vehicle was now totally out of control and I knew we weren't going to brake in time. We were going to hit the tree at a speed of over 50 miles per hour.

I spun back round again to discover that Tabitha had opened her seatbelt and was in the process of climbing out of her car seat. She would almost certainly go through the window. She was already halfway out of her seatbelt, crying her eyes out and screaming at the top of her voice. I had to make an instant decision: either try and strap her back in again whilst my own seatbelt was undone or bring her into the front with me. In a split-second I hauled her into the front and put the seatbelt around us both. Then I put my feet up on the dashboard and shut my eyes.

As the impact happened I straightened my legs to take the full force of it. The massive jolt shot through my legs and body and I felt the seatbelt tighten and pain sear across my right shoulder and breast. Glass shattered everywhere.

As soon as we stopped I unclipped the belt with the intention of getting out of the car and away from all the wreckage as quickly as possible. Then I realized my daughter wasn't breathing very well and was making choking noises. She was struggling to get air. Then, terrifyingly, she stopped breathing completely!

I was panic stricken. I screamed at the top of my lungs, 'Someone help my baby! Please, someone help her!' over and over again.

Suddenly a dark-haired lady appeared from nowhere with a blanket. I was puzzled as to where she might have come from. When I asked her, she indicated a nearby house.

Just then, an ambulance appeared from over the hill. Then I became aware of another car, a white car, which had stopped, and I saw a phone in the hand of the person in it, so I assumed they had phoned for an ambulance. The police then appeared also, but I was too intent on what was happening with my daughter to take in many details. All this while, though, the dark-haired lady who had been soothing Tabitha and who had brought her a blanket was calmly singing and hovering her hand over her chest.

I had never felt so helpless in my life! I could still hear my own voice begging and pleading for help. Then the back doors of the ambulance were flung open and the paramedics were there. My shoulder and breast were agony, but I handed my daughter over to them and climbed into the back of the ambulance along with her. I watched them rip her clothes off, hook the monitors up to her and give her oxygen.

In a panic I turned to the dark-haired woman and asked who she was. 'I am a nurse,' she replied. 'Your daughter, she will live, don't worry.'

I wanted to stop and speak to her, but the doors of the ambulance closed rapidly and the sound of the siren started blaring in the background. My husband remained at the scene, unaware if his daughter was alive or dead.

A huge team of paramedics and paediatric consultants was waiting for us when we drew up outside the hospital. I was told to wait in the relatives' room as my daughter was whisked into the emergency room. As she was taken away, I just caught sight of her eyes as they closed in a look of sheer terror. I didn't know if I would see my baby alive again. The agony of waiting seemed eternal.

Eventually a nurse came to get me and asked me to go with her. I ran up the corridor and burst into the emergency room. My little girl was lying there with her head turned to the wall. My heart stopped. Was she ...? No! Suddenly, her head turned to me and she called out, 'Mummy!' and put her little hand out to me. I just ran to her.

The doctor told me, 'She is one very lucky little lady. We thought she was a "gonner", but she suddenly stabilized. She will have to be kept in for a few days for observation, but we are hopeful she will make a full recovery.'

'Can I touch her?' I asked.

'Of course. She could probably do with a cuddle.'

I was so grateful. The doctors and the police said that if I hadn't hauled my daughter into the front with me she would most certainly have gone through the windscreen and been

> killed. I had taken the full impact on my legs and this had saved her life. (My legs were massively bruised but not broken. My right shoulder and breast were bruised so badly that even I didn't recognize my own body, but otherwise I was OK.)
>
> The strange thing was that I still had the blanket that the woman had wrapped around my baby to keep her warm, but no one else at the accident had even seen her. Afterwards I went back to the area, but I never found the owner of the blanket. So I still have it – and the reassurance she gave me. That woman had cared for my baby and soothed her and wrapped her to keep her warm. I think I just might have had the privilege of meeting my daughter's guardian angel!

Safely Steering

I think this next story has a little guardian angel attached to it too:

> My late parents lived in a bungalow with a curved drive that carried on to the bottom of a slope and ended at a kerb. One day as they turned into the drive going down the slope the brakes of their car failed. Although the car was not going very fast, my father, who was driving, realized that without following the drive completely they would smash into a large glass window in the building at the bottom of the drive.

As he reached the end of the drive, to avoid going over the kerb, he made a split-second decision (which he never understood) to turn the steering wheel to the right, which took the car between a large brick wall and a waist-high wall on the left. In between was a set of about 10 concrete steps ending in a playground. Both my parents say they closed their eyes as they went between the walls and opened them as the car stopped. When they opened their eyes again the car had come to a complete stop and it was totally intact. Neither of them could believe it, as the car appeared to be much wider than the gap they seemed to have driven through.

After they had calmed down my parents fetched a tape measure to measure the gap, which actually proved to be narrower than the car itself. Also, a mechanic they asked to look at the car confirmed that the brakes were still not working! Neither of them had felt the car going down any steps, only feeling it stop at the bottom.

It's a real mystery, but my mother always claimed she called out to angels as she closed her eyes. She always believed in them!

A Car Warning and Seeing a Brother

Elizabeth is from Australia. She can recall two different occasions when she felt her angels were with her.

She explained. 'The first time I was driving to work and it was dark. It was 6 a.m. and the car coming towards me was overtaking another car.'

The car shot past Elizabeth in the middle of the road and gave her a bit of a shock because it seemed to come so close. She recalls:

> I had to brake really hard and I was pretty shaken up, but then when I looked again, there were no cars on the road at all. I know I hadn't imagined it, but I've no idea where the cars had suddenly disappeared to!

What had Elizabeth seen? She was confused. She told me, 'I thanked my angel and proceeded on my journey.'

Elizabeth wondered if the experience was a sign of some sort. Maybe it meant she should slow down? She decided she would slow down just in case.

Moments later the same scenario was playing itself out in front of her for real:

> A car was now doing exactly what I had seen in my vision, except this time I was ready! I realized that my angels had given me notice so that I could be prepared, and because I had seen what was about to happen, I managed to brake in plenty of time and move out of the way safely. I really felt that without the forewarning I would have been involved in a serious accident.

Elizabeth remembered to thank her angels again for the warning.

This wasn't the only close angelic encounter that she had in the car:

> A few months later I was driving home from work. It was a sunny afternoon and I was taking my time, enjoying the view around me. I realized I was probably going a bit too slowly for the other drivers and was just about to speed up when I heard a loud *'No!'* in my head. Sure enough, a white van was overtaking on a bend and I was able to avert the accident! The angels had helped me once again!

Elizabeth's experiences weren't just simple feelings. In the first experience she actually saw a vision and in the second she heard a physical voice, something that isn't so easy to ignore. She firmly believes that the voice was sent to help her and that it was probably the same energy that had protected her during her earlier experience.

She says, 'If I had been driving at the correct speed, I might not be here today, so I thanked my angels again!'

As well as these angelic encounters, Elizabeth has had other magical experiences:

> My brother Arthur passed away when I was 12 and he came to me in a vision on that very night to say his good-byes. I will never forget that.
>
> Then, when my dad passed away four years ago, I was lucky to be with him as he crossed over. He told me that his

mother and sister (who had passed years before), had come to collect him. I watched the joy on Dad's face. It was overwhelming.

Seeing a dying person being collected is a familiar experience to many of those who are lucky enough to be with their loved ones when their time comes.

Elizabeth explained, 'Even though it was such a sad occasion, there was also tremendous joy.'

There are more stories like this later in the book. In the meantime, remember to ask your own guardian angel to be with you when you drive. I remember an advert that was on TV once for a well-known brand of car. It showed angels, complete with wings, sitting in the car or flying with people as they were driving around. Of course this particular car was supposed to be so safe that the owner didn't need her angel with her whilst she drove.

I guess I will keep asking my own angel to be with me just in case!

Nowhere Left to Go

Gillian once had an amazing experience in the car. She calls it 'the one thing my mum and I will never be able to forget – or explain'.

At the time Gillian was living in Germany and on this particular day she was travelling with her mother and a friend to Bergen-Belsen, where the young Jewish diarist Anne Frank died.

Gillian explains:

> I was driving and my friend was in the front and my mum was sitting behind me. I was driving along the autobahn at around 110 miles an hour. In Germany they drive their cars very fast compared to many other parts of the world.

Gillian was very comfortable with the speed, however, and there seemed no obvious danger at the time. Gillian's was the lead car:

> There were only two lanes of traffic. I was nearly level with the car in the other lane when all of a sudden a car came from nowhere and went to overtake me! There was no room for her to go past and I should have hit the other car right in the middle.

Gillian remembers swearing very loudly in her head and thinking, 'That driver has just killed me!' There seemed no safe outcome for the drivers around either and in that fraction of a second, Gillian felt her time was up.

> I put the brakes on, even though at the time I thought it was pointless. I couldn't imagine how it would be able to help. However, instead of hitting the other car, as I'd felt was inevitable, we were now in the middle lane and cars were

> overtaking us and looking at us to see if we were alright. I had no idea how we had got there or what had happened. It's as if time had slowed down somehow. I looked in front of me and spotted the other driver going over a hill – miles in front of us.

All three drivers were shaken up by what had just happened. As Gillian said,

> My mum just told me to pull over at the next exit, which I did. We both said, 'Did you see that?' My friend who was sitting in the front had not seen anything and she thought I was over-reacting. It was as if she had been protected from the anxiety of what we had just experienced. Perhaps she had been asleep or something, because she had seemed to be slumped in the front, as if someone, or something, had just switched her off. In fact I think if she had been aware, we would have been killed, because she would have certainly tried to grab the wheel of the car.

Although Gillian is still not completely sure what happened, she said:

> One thing is for sure – we were not meant to die that day. The whole event has affected my life so much. Since that time, I have become a healer and my belief in angels has become a lot stronger.

Gillian's story has much in common with other stories I have received over the years. People often know that something dramatic has happened to them, but find it hard to explain what or how it could have occurred. Cars are moved, lifted and even change direction without any explanation. Sometimes time seems to stand still and at other times it appears to be missing entirely, even if only for a few seconds. Are angels standing guard, waiting to lift us out of danger? I believe they are.

Safe in the Fog – the Angel Satellite Navigation System

This next story comes from Sheena, who has a real mystery to share with us. Her angels were on hand to help a young girl out of clear danger on the roads. Was her angel working like a modern-day satellite navigation system to guide her in her car? Let's look at her story.

Sheena told me about two incidents. She said:

> The first incident happened when I was about 18 years old. I had recently started a new job and the drive to work was a little complicated. I had to drive down a series of country lanes and I wasn't very familiar with them at all.

Sheena was nervous on her drive to work, so when evening came around and she had to drive back again she was already anxious:

> On the way home it became very foggy. It was hopeless and I simply didn't have a clue where I was going. I remember just watching the white line along the side of the road to make sure I was even staying on the road. It would have been very easy to take a wrong turn, hit another car or just to end up upside down in a ditch.

Sheena was at her wits' end, but then, in no time at all, she found herself in a familiar town. It was well lit and Sheena recognized it. What a relief! At least now she knew she would be able to find her way home. But strangely the town was nowhere near where she had thought she was driving and she had absolutely no idea how on earth she had got there! Even without the fog, she says she would never have managed to get herself to this town travelling the route she had – or thought she had!

Sheena was bemused, but the rest of the journey went without incident and she soon found herself safely at home.

Her parents had been worried and were waiting up for her when she got home. They too were totally bemused by the route she must have taken:

My dad got the map out to see how I got to the town because he knows his way around so well. But he couldn't make any sense of it and said the only way would have been if I had cut through a field. He had no idea how I had driven along country lanes and found my way there.

The whole thing was a complete mystery. Even after all this time Sheena still remembers it well. Perhaps it was an angel who guided her? She thinks it might be.

Although this isn't car related, Sheena did have another strange experience which might have involved an angel. She told me:

When I was in my early twenties I was going on a night out with my friends. I was walking to the meeting-place on my own when I suddenly became aware of a man walking behind me. Initially I didn't think much about it, as he was a safe distance away. But then I had to walk along a dark path and when I got to the top of it, in my head I heard, 'Run!' I didn't have to be told twice and I ran as fast as I could until I got back onto a lit street.

What had happened here? Was this just an imaginary worry or was the voice real? Sheena said:

At first I thought that maybe I was just being paranoid, but when I got back onto a lit street I suddenly realized that the guy wasn't far behind me. And the only way he could have kept up was by running too. That really made me think!

At the time I never really questioned the voice that I'd heard. I mean, it never occurred to me that I might have had some help from 'another source'. To be honest, I had forgotten about both incidents until I was reading your book *An Angel Saved my Life* and then the memories just came right back to me. I think angels were showing me when they had been there for me, and I was amazed, because I hadn't even been trying to think of particular experiences. I'd thought I was just reading a book!

I wonder if the mystery voice was the same angel who had helped with the car incident?

An Angel Feather Sign

This next story is going to sound a little familiar – another overtaking scenario rears its ugly head. I think we can see how some of our most dangerous situations come about whilst driving …

Belinda explains:

Several years ago, just out of curiosity really, I visited a fair which had various stalls about alternative healing, crystals, aromatherapy, *feng shui*, etc. I was drawn to the pure beauty of the crystals and started my own collection, which has grown considerably over the years. I also became interested in books about angels and faeries and I regularly ask angels for help in finding parking spaces. I have lost count of the number of times my children, and even my husband, have mocked me and say, 'Oh, it's just coincidence,' but now even they say to me, 'Why don't you ask the fairies, Mum?' I think they mean the angels!

Last year we were planning a special Sunday family day out. As I was going to get into the car I noticed a pure white feather nestling in the windscreen. I immediately thought of my angel friend and said, 'Oh, so you want to come along for the day too?' I picked up the feather and put it on the inside of the car windscreen before we drove off.

The family started off on their journey, but it wasn't long before the peace was shattered. Belinda takes up the story:

Going along a straight road which is about a mile and a half long I was shocked to see that an articulated lorry was overtaking a small car and was heading straight for us.

My children screamed and my husband shouted something, but I never panicked for one moment, and I don't know how, but the lorry managed to pass us completely. We never had a scratch on the car. The whole thing seemed to happen as if someone else was holding the steering wheel – as if someone else was driving, even.

Someone else took the wheel? Invisible hands maybe, but was it angels? Belinda says:

> I know that angels were sitting in the car with us that day. I say to my husband, 'You know that white feather? It was an angel on our side,' and his reply is always, 'I'm not going to argue with you on that one!'

Belinda still finds lots of white feathers:

> I used to collect them. Sometimes I still do, but whenever I am walking my dog and I see them, I always smile and say, 'Hello.' I think it's the angels' way of letting me know they're around.

'Angels Wake Me'

Although there is no 'proof' that the gentleman in this next story was in any danger, I thought I would add his story here to show the full extent of the angels-in-the-car phenomenon and how angels in fact appear to watch over us in all kinds of transport. Dave had the following experiences whilst working in New York:

> In 1992 I was working in Manhattan and living on Staten Island. After a long day's work I would often go for a few drinks then start the long journey home, which would entail a subway train from mid Manhattan to lower Manhattan,

where I would get the ferry across to Staten Island before catching a bus halfway round the island to where I was living.

On a few occasions I fell asleep on the ferry and ended up waking just as we were docking back at Manhatten. Once I fell asleep on the bus and woke up well past my stop and ended up having to travel right round the island to get back home.

This happened twice more, once on the ferry and once on the bus, but on these occasions there was a difference. The first time I fell asleep again, but was woken up by a male voice calling my name as clear as day. I looked round and nobody was anywhere near me. Then I realized that I had been woken just as the ferry was docking at Staten Island. At the time I didn't put too much thought into it, but I was glad I had woken up.

The second time this happened a male voice called my name again. This time I was on the bus about 500 yards from my stop. It was so real that I looked around to see who had woken me and again there was no one.

Eventually I came to the conclusion that it was my guardian angel. It certainly got my attention.

I welcome the contact anytime so that I don't miss my stop – every little helps!

Missed the Tram ...

That last story showed an angel being quite helpful, but this next one is a lot more dramatic. Sometimes the inevitable *doesn't* happen and we are left wondering why! Is it angels at work? Mary thinks so. She is from Australia. She told me:

> I had just obtained my driver's licence and like any young person I liked to drive a little faster than I should have. This one particular night I had just finished work and was on my way home. I was waiting for the lights to turn green at a very busy intersection. As soon as they changed, I put my foot down and drove off.
>
> What happened next is still a big puzzle to me. All I remember is turning into a busy road, losing control of the car and going across the opposite side of the road against all the oncoming traffic.
>
> At this point I shut my eyes tight, hoping that when I opened them again I would discover the whole thing had been a dream. But it wasn't. I was shocked to see a tram coming straight towards me.
>
> Now this is where the miracle comes in, because I thought to myself, 'I am going to die,' and I closed my eyes and said, 'Oh my God, please help me.'
>
> The next thing I remember was opening my eyes and being amazed. My car had somehow managed to bypass all the traffic, totally missed the tram and ended up on the

sidewalk on the opposite side of the road! The only thing that had stopped me from going through the brick wall was a 'NO STANDING' sign. My car didn't even have a scratch on it. Thank goodness that there were no pedestrians walking by when my car came crashing through.

I can't believe I'm here telling you this story. It still puzzles me. But I believe that my guardian angel saved me. I guess it just wasn't my time to go.

CHAPTER 3

Angels of Healing

But if these beings guard you, they do so because they have been summoned by your prayers.

Ambrose

Angels seem to hang around a lot at hospitals or come close to us when we are sick, depressed or need emotional healing. Many of the following stories relate to angels or deceased loved ones appearing when we are scared or our lives are in danger. We see our angels sitting on the end of the bed, or they appear in dreams. Sometimes we see them when we are unconscious or shortly before or after an operation. Our angels are around to reassure us and help to save our lives. Their job is to protect us and watch over us. Many religions and cultures around the world believe in God's angels in one form or another.

Many hospital stories that people share with me include the 'mysterious' nurse, doctor or hospital visitor who sits by the bed or appears each day. The strange thing is that no one else can see this devoted figure (not usually, anyway). As soon as we are well again they disappear into the night as if they had never been there at all.

When we are in an altered state of consciousness, sleeping or even unconscious, strangely enough it is easier for our celestial friends to reach out to us. It's at this time that we are most likely to see them. Don't ever think that this is the only time that they are around us, though. Our winged angels and our special loved ones in heaven are always with us, working quietly in the background. They always have our best interests in mind – even if we don't always feel they do. They help where they can – sometimes when they are not supposed to! They love us and support us in more ways than you can imagine.

Sometimes we recognize our special helpers as people we have known in the past and at other times we don't recognize our saviours at all. However, as already mentioned, even when angels try to visit us 'in disguise', they nearly always give themselves away by their unusual appearance. Of course the wings are a dead giveaway, but not everyone is lucky enough to see them. I do believe they show them more for our benefit than their own!

I'd like to share some special stories with you.

Rose Quartz Comfort

Susan is from England and the events in her story happened a couple of years ago. It concerned her father, who passed over in 1972. She wrote to me:

> I'm in the habit of wearing a pink rose quartz stone next to my skin – in my bra! I'd read somewhere that wearing one next to or near the heart was calming and this proved to be the case with me. So it had been a habit for quite some time, a year or more, to wear a rose quartz crystal like that. I'd worn it for so long in fact, I felt 'undressed' without it.
>
> This particular day after work I went clothes shopping. I'd seen a couple of tops I liked, so popped into the fitting room to try them on.
>
> I always change out of my work clothes when I get home and that day was no different. That's when I noticed the rose quartz had gone. I imagine it had slipped out of my bra in the changing room.
>
> It may sound strange, but I was quite distraught over this, as I had definitely felt more peaceful and calm since wearing the rose quartz. I hunted high and low in the house, but knew in my heart that it would be sitting on the floor of the changing room.
>
> A couple of days passed and I still I felt upset at losing the crystal. It wasn't an easy thing to replace, either, because it meant driving into the next town to buy another one.

Then in the evening just after 9 p.m. I was sitting on the sofa with my feet up and the lights off when all of a sudden I heard something drop just by my legs onto the floor. It sounded similar to what a stone might sound like when dropped onto a wooden floor. I looked to see what it could be and there, right by the sofa, was my rose quartz stone! It just seemed to have dropped out of midair! I knew it hadn't been there before because I have the wooden flooring that is so popular now and I would have definitely seen or walked on it in the days since I'd lost it.

I couldn't believe my eyes and absolutely knew my dad had picked up my vibes and found it and delivered it back to me. I felt so emotional that tears came to my eyes, thanks to the wondrous knowledge that my dad was in the room with me. Although I couldn't see him, I just felt him there with me.

Since then I have lost this stone again and had to replace it with a new one. Months later I found it again, though, on my garden path. It was lying there as clear as day. There is no way I could have missed it before if it had lain there for months. My dad at work again!

I loved this story and it reminded me of a similar experience of my own when I'd lost one of a pair of gold hooped earrings that I'd been given as an eighteenth birthday present and had asked my angels if they would try and find it for me. The next morning there it was, lying on the windowsill with the other one!

Isn't it strange how our angels and angelic loved ones can do these things? I guess in the future we'll have a scientific explanation for it, but for now it's just a little bit of magic!

A Visit from an Angel during an Operation

Sue isn't someone who likes to draw attention to herself. In fact when she first shared her story with me I wanted to include it in a magazine article and she asked to remain anonymous – as she does here. Sue *is* her real name, though. She is in her forties, but of course she could live anywhere in the whole world and I'll let that bit be our 'little secret'!

Sue wrote to me after searching the internet for information about angels. So many people around the world have experienced these special beings of light and want to discover a little more, and the internet can be the perfect way of finding out. Sue is one of these people and was kind enough to share her own special angel visit with me.

It all began with a trip to hospital. She told me, 'I hadn't been well for over a year and after many hospital visits they discovered I had a large fibroid which had to be removed.'

Sue wasn't worried, as she had already been to hospital a few times for similar operations. The hospital was familiar to her and she wasn't particularly concerned about the operation itself.

Strangely, however, on the morning of the operation, just an hour before she was due to have her fibroid removed, Sue felt the urge to walk down to the pay phone and ring her husband and her mother. Something felt different this time and when she walked back to her bed after making her calls, she had the strangest feeling that she had just said goodbye to her loved ones. An ominous cloud descended on her and she found it hard to shake it off. She explained:

> I'm normally such a positive person and I was worried that I was thinking like that, so in my mind I asked for the spirits of my deceased father and brother to look after me. I just wanted to know that someone was watching out for me.

Sue went ahead with the operation and just a few hours later woke up to find herself back on the ward with her husband by her side. As she opened her eyes she said hello to her husband and then something distracted her over by the window. She was stunned, she told me, to see 'a beautiful male angel' looking in her direction.

The angel began to move away almost immediately and in a panic Sue asked him to stay, but he told her, 'You don't need me anymore. You are OK,' and with that he simply flew away!

Right away Sue told her husband about her vision, but he simply laughed and put it down to the medication. But Sue already felt so much better she was ready to get up. The nurses told her, 'You must stay in bed,' but she had other ideas: 'I told them I realized I had been cut from one side of my hip to the other and it did hurt to move, but I still felt so well!'

In fact she was moving about so quickly after the operation that it soon became clear to everyone that something unusual had happened.

The next morning Sue had a phone call from the surgeon:

> He asked me how I was and if he could come and see me. I got up, washed and waited. When he came to the ward he was quite excited and seemed genuinely surprised to see me up and about. I told him, 'I feel so well.'
>
> He explained that the surgical team had actually removed a 12lb fibroid that had been attached to my organs and spine. It had been so big that it had had to be cut away a little at a time. The surgeon told me they had all been amazed at how well I had been functioning once they had opened me up and seen the size of the fibroid.
>
> It was what he said next that really surprised me: 'By rights you shouldn't have been so well. Someone has been watching over you.'
>
> I laughed to myself and thought, 'If only you knew about my angel!'

The surgeon had made a throwaway comment, but in fact the angel had been there the whole time watching over Sue. No wonder she had felt so well – she had experienced a little *divine intervention*!

Angel Blessings

This next story is from writer Michelle Jones. She told me:

> I suppose I would describe myself as a sceptical believer. Just because I've had psychic and paranormal experiences throughout my life doesn't mean that I accept everything at face value. In fact I like to thoroughly investigate each experience to try to find a 'rational' explanation. Some things, however, defy that rational interpretation.

In October 2004, Michelle was given the horrific news that she had breast cancer. After treatment, she says:

> Although my physical body was recovering (I am now recovered and clear, God willing), my psychic and spiritual self was in trouble. I felt cut off and abandoned.

But Michelle hadn't been abandoned and had an unusual visitation shortly afterwards. She told me:

> One night in June 2005 I awoke around 2.30 a.m. to see what appeared to be two glowing heads floating next to the bedroom wall about six feet away from me. They were

each about the size of a football and had glowing tendrils waving away underneath them (a bit like a jellyfish). As we always have a window and a curtain open at night and there is a streetlight that shines through the window, I immediately assumed that this was an effect caused by light and shadows through the net curtains. However, I was having difficulties with sorting out in my head how these images were made up and so in the end I had to get up and really look.

Michelle was totally confused, as most people would be:

First I went over to the windows and wiggled the curtains about and then I tried opening the window further or shutting it completely. This did not have any effect, so I returned to my side of the bed and discovered, to my amazement, that the heads appeared to be three-dimensional! Still, I wondered if maybe I was not fully awake, so I nipped off to the bathroom, turned the light on to make sure I was definitely conscious and then returned to the bedroom. The heads were still there! I stood and stared at them for some time and although I could not make out any features, I was given the impression that these were faces looking back at me. At no time was I afraid of these glowing faces; in fact I felt quite at ease.

Eventually Michelle went back to bed and to sleep. Nothing else happened that night.

> The following night I woke up again around the same time, but this time there was no sign of the phenomenon and I could not recreate it by twitching the curtain or moving things around to create shadows.

But this wasn't the end of the story:

> I saw the heads on one more occasion and then a couple of nights later I woke up and found them hovering near the wall above my head! I do believe that these were angels sent to reassure me that I would regain my connections to spirit and to my psychic senses. It was a relief to know that I was not alone during this time.
>
> Since those memorable few nights in June, I feel as though I have suddenly signed up for a sort of 'spiritual broadband', having been on 'dial up' all these years!
>
> I would like to pass on this message to others who are dealing with difficult times in their lives. Angels and those in spirit are always watching over us and if you ask for help it will be given, though you may need to listen for the reply.

Thanks, Michelle! I couldn't have put it better myself. It's great to know that when she needed that support in her life she was literally shown that she was not alone. And isn't it strange that people seem unafraid of any sort of angelic light formation? You would automatically assume that fear would be a part of the experience, but I've discovered that it rarely is.

'An Angel Held My Hand'

Susan is from England. She lost her lovely dad in March 1972. His death was very unexpected. She shared her story with me:

Dad was only 55 when he died. I was married at the time, but it was before my children came along. My son, Jon, was born two years later and my daughter, Nicky, followed in 1978.

The birth of my daughter was not an easy one. The doctors decided that I needed to have an emergency Caesarean and after 12 hours of labour I was ready to be knocked out, but something went terribly wrong and I didn't lose consciousness straight away. I've since learned this was a common occurrence at that time. I remember a nurse checking my eyelids and saying I was out, but I wasn't. I desperately tried to convey to her with my eyes that I was totally aware of what was happening, but she didn't understand because I was immobilized by relaxant drugs. I actually felt the scalpel slice me open and it was the most horrific pain I'd ever felt in my entire life. It was so unbelievably severe that I remember praying to God for death and so oblivion – anything to get away from the pain.

That's when it happened. Suddenly everything went black. I seemed to be drawn into a swirling tunnel with strange music and almost immediately I was aware of my dad speaking to me. I could feel his presence and was stunned that I was meeting up with him again. I remember asking him for proof of the afterlife and also asking him if he was happy.

Dad provided the proof with the words to a popular song at that time. Don't ask me how I knew, but I was certain the words were correct and we sang the song together and somehow were accompanied by the music too! Other proofs were provided, as well.

But no sooner had we met up then it was over. I was back in the tunnel again, but this time I was being drawn back out. I could once again hear the strange tunnel music and then I was aware of the nurse leaning over me and checking my eyelids and trying to bring me round. She kept telling me that I had a beautiful baby daughter, but I was unable to react to the news. It felt as though she was on the other side of a veil – close yet far away.

Then I was aware that Dad was walking beside me as they were wheeling me out of the theatre. I could feel him holding my hand as he was walking beside the trolley. I was in so much pain that I was pleading with him to let me go with him, but I knew I was being sent back. Then it felt that I had been 'pinged' back to reality and right away he was gone. And for the life of me I couldn't remember the words to the song or what the other proofs had been.

The nurse was still trying to bring me round by telling me about my daughter. Apparently the medical staff had been aware that I had been 'somewhere else' and she asked me who I had been talking to. I told her it was my dad who had passed over some years before. The look on her face was priceless!

This was the beginning of many spiritual wonders concerning my dad. I am closer to him now than I was at any time during his lifetime and when I'm going through rough patches and want answers I know he will come to me either in dreams or I will feel his presence around me, which gives me a lovely glow and feeling of great peace.

I'll never forget the day my special 'angel' held my hand.

Smoking Can Kill

This next 'angel' was a little more forceful than most. This story is from Gillian in Germany:

I once read that we have free will, but maybe not in everything.

I gave up smoking a few years back and then shortly afterwards started up again. My mum wasn't happy that I'd started smoking again. She thought I was stupid! One Sunday she was over and she just looked at me and said, 'You will die if you don't give up smoking. You know that "upstairs" isn't happy.' (I guess she meant God.) She seemed so serious, but I told her that the choice was mine and I could smoke if I wanted to.

Well, I went to light up a cigarette and I could not put it to my lips – it just would not go. Then I started to cough. I have no idea what happened, but it was as if someone or something was stopping me from smoking. I have not smoked since and in fact I cannot stand the smell of it now and I cough when someone is smoking near me.

What's funny is that a short while later I didn't sleep very well one night. I was actually awake for most of it. Then when I did finally get some sleep, when I woke up I couldn't move my left side at all. That actually happened two mornings in a row and it made me think that if I had still been smoking, the paralysis might have been permanent.

I guess it is a good idea to have a forceful angel after all!

Healing Arms

This next story is about another forceful angel. Patricia is from England and her angel appeared 'in disguise' …

My story begins nearly 30 years ago when I was 14. It was a difficult time in my life and for reasons I'm not still clear about I decided to try to end my life. Instead of going to school as usual I walked several miles from my home until I reached a small village with a little shop. From the shop I purchased a bottle of painkillers and proceeded to swallow the whole bottle of 50 with a can of coke.

I now know that 10 can kill and that 50 was most certainly a lethal dose unless I received help pretty quickly.

Afterwards I pondered on what to do whilst I was waiting to die. At this point I looked to the heavens and spoke to

God. Although I wasn't religious, I told God that I would soon be joining him and asked him to look after me.

As I continued down the deserted village road a car pulled up beside me and the man inside asked me if I was alright. I replied that I was and continued on my way, but he was very persistent and asked if I would like a lift. Now at 14 I knew all about the dangers of getting in the cars of strangers, but I had the feeling that I could trust this man. What had I got to lose? I'd already planned on killing myself anyway!

Once I was inside the car he told me that he was a doctor and was on his way to work. Then I knew I had to tell him what I had taken.

Needless to say, he took me to hospital, where I had my stomach pumped and was put on a drip. Happily, I made a full recovery.

Over the years I've often thought about my experience and wondered what the odds were that a doctor would be passing down that road at that particular time. Even more astonishing was the fact that he actually stopped the car and I accepted his lift!

I suspect that someone was watching over me that day and it was most certainly not my time to go. I really believe that the doctor was my angel. Was he human? He must have been inspired by angels if he wasn't one himself!

Patricia had another strange experience following the very sad death of her brother-in-law, who died at the young age of 42. She wrote:

His death came as a great shock to the whole family and made me question my own mortality. I began asking questions about the afterlife, which I've since discussed with my daughter. I started to reflect on my own experience of 30 years ago and wondered if my own guardian angel was still looking after me. I decided to ask my angel to give me some sort of sign.

What happened next truly astounded me. I drifted off to sleep and then in the early hours of the morning I was woken by someone saying my name as clearly as anything. It felt as if my name had been spoken in a loud whisper right into my ear. Then I felt as though two gigantic arms were wrapping themselves around my whole body, just as they might have done if I were a small child. These arms cuddled me in a comforting way and then lifted me up the bed as if to make me more comfortable. All the time I was awake but my eyes remained shut.

I felt the arms withdraw and then was able to open my eyes. I could see my husband was fast asleep with his back turned to me, so I knew it couldn't have been him – and besides the arms had been huge. I was lying on my side and really wanted to look in the direction from which the voice and arms had come, but for some reason I could not.

As the gradual realization of what had happened dawned on me, I realized that this was the sign I had asked for. I just lay awake for a while feeling incredibly calm and relaxed and then I fell asleep again.

The next morning I excitedly told my husband what I had experienced and to be honest, I was convinced that he would think I had gone mad. Surprisingly, he accepted what I said, saying he believed me.

A lot of people would say that it must have been a dream, but I know it was real. I heard that voice and felt those arms and just know it was my angel telling me that I was being looked after.

Loving Visitors from the Other Side

Here is another story from England. Laura dropped me an e-mail about her experiences. She wrote:

I had several experiences as a child, but my most recent experience was very exciting. In August 2005 I was rushed into the Queen Elizabeth Hospital in Birmingham because I had become very ill with auto-immune hepatitis. I can't remember much about the time itself, but I remember that before I was diagnosed I knew I was very ill. Strangely, I kept seeing my grandmother and grandfather, who had crossed over years before.

When I was finally diagnosed, they told me I was top priority for a liver transplant. I hadn't realized the severity of the situation until they told my family that I would die if I didn't get the transplant. We were all very shocked. Later my family told me that at one point I had been given only hours to live! At the time I had had no idea.

That evening I sat in the bath, feeling very low and scared. Whilst I was in there, a white feather floated down in a shaft of light – lovely, but as this happened I vomited! I rang my sister-in-law and she calmed me and said the feather was a sign from my guardian angel that everything was going to be OK.

At 11 p.m. I relaxed and had a vision of a beautiful garden. Whilst I was in this beautiful place, one of the nurses sat with me holding my hand. She was a lady from Jamaica and I remember her so clearly. She had the most beautiful smile and we spoke of my wedding there and talked about my two beautiful boys.

Then one of the doctors came through and told me that they had a match for my transplant – just like that. From that point on I only have a few memories and it didn't seem long before I was well enough to go home.

The second night at home, I lay listening to my two boys breathing in their sleep and I felt so blessed to be home with them. My dog Benji seemed worried about me, though, and sat staring at me with his paw on my arm all night, so I didn't sleep much.

Then the next day I had the most wonderful dream/vision. First I was back in that amazing garden. I could smell and see beautiful flowers like lily of the valley

the other side and part of the souls of my family still on the Earth are with me, supporting me through my life challenges. We truly are never alone.

Healing Angels

Janet comes from Australia. She believes that her angels helped her with her healing and I'm sure she's right!

After I had been ill for some time, my doctor decided that maybe an ultrasound test would help uncover the problem. As a result of the test they discovered lots of gallstones and that there were many hanging on the top of the bile duct. This could be a serious problem if they were to go into the bile duct itself.

I'm a firm believer in guardian angels, so right away I started asking my angels to please help take the stones away and make my body well again. I really believed that this would happen and trusted with my heart that the stones would be removed.

Well, after a few months I went back to the doctor and had more tests. He shook his head in confusion and said he couldn't believe it. There were no stones to be seen! They had simply disappeared.

Now every day I thank my angels for keeping me well and I talk to them and thank them for taking care of me and my family. I know it was more than just a coincidence.

'Say My Name ...'

Sian is from Wales and she has been aware of her angel for a while, but always wanted to know its name:

I have believed in God and angels for as long as I can remember and I recently went through a health scare and found comfort in knowing that I was not alone. I would find white feathers everywhere and my family and friends noticed this too. I believe that the feathers were a sign from my angels. After the all-clear from the hospital I began reading as many books on angels and the afterlife as I could find and I found that I became an even stronger afterlife and angel believer.

A few months ago I meditated and asked for my guardian angel's name and kept seeing the name 'Peter'. I asked for confirmation and nothing happened for three days, so I forgot about it. Then a strange thing happened. My husband and I were watching a film and we decided to order a takeaway. The boy in the shop asked me for all of our information and then he asked me for my password. Like most people, we use the same password for everything, so I gave it, but he said, 'No, the password is Peter!' He told me that it had been changed a few days ago! I was totally dumbstruck, but over the moon. Mind you, it did freak out my husband.

All Better Now on the Other Side

Diane is from Manchester. She writes:

Early in 1987 my mum had major surgery for bowel cancer. Unfortunately it was too late and she passed away on 11 May that year.

I was devastated, as my father had not told me the hospice had phoned him saying that Mum did not have long left and that he should go to her. He didn't make it in time and I always thought that she would have been by herself when she died. I felt as though I had a heavy weight on my shoulders and like many people I felt so guilty for not being with my mother in her last moments on Earth.

The day of her birthday I woke up to the strong smell of roses. Halfway down the stairs it stopped. I'd go back up a stair and the smell was there again, then back down one stair and it was gone. It was very strange, but I really felt that Mum had come to visit! I wished her a happy birthday and put some flowers in the kitchen for her.

Diane was comforted by the experience, but still grieving:

For two years I struggled to come to terms with what had happened and got upset quite easily. Then one night when I was in bed I was also aware of being awake and standing downstairs in the front room by the fire. My mum was sitting on the sofa smiling at me and the corner of the room seemed to open up and I could see a very bright light out of the corner of my eye. I could also sense someone standing by the light.

I went over to my mum and as I did so I looked back and I could see myself standing on the rug by the fire watching everything that was going on!

I sat next to my mother, put my arms around her shoulders and asked, 'Are you OK, Mum? Are you better now?'

She looked up at the person who was with her and he said to her, 'Dorothy, you *are* better now,' and she replied, 'Am I?' and he answered, 'Yes, you are better now!' With that she turned and looked at me and smiled and immediately they were gone.

I woke up right away and sat up in bed. I knew the experience had been real. It had been unlike anything I had ever experienced in my life before.

Since then, the weight I felt has lifted completely and I can smile at the thought that my mother is OK. The light I saw was so beautiful and felt so calming. When I told a friend she said that it was my mind telling me I wanted my mum to come back. Why do people do that? I know it was real.

A Kiss of Support

Here is another experience from England. This is Carol's story:

I went through a very difficult time in my life after my husband left me and our two children and I just didn't know which way to turn. This particular night I went to bed as normal and I was just about to fall asleep when I felt someone very gently sit on the bottom of the bed. I thought I had left the cat in, so I moved my leg across the bottom of the bed to get him off, but he wasn't there. I moved down the bed and slid my leg back, but still there was no one there. Then, spookily, after a few minutes I felt someone move off the bed!

When I woke the next morning the cat was sitting waiting on the doorstep as usual, so I knew for sure it hadn't been him, but I wasn't too sure who it had been. It hadn't been scary, though, and to be honest I found the whole thing a comfort.

After a few years of being on my own I met a wonderful man. After a while I could tell things were getting serious and I was terrified because I didn't want to be hurt again. One night I had settled down in bed when I was once again aware there was someone in the room with me. I tried to open my eyes, but I couldn't. Then I started to sense whoever was in the room with me had begun to move around the bed towards me. It sounds scary, but it honestly wasn't. I could feel them getting closer then I knew they were right at my side, which was strange in itself as they had 'walked' through the empty side of the bed to get to me. I then felt whoever it was put their arms around me and kiss me on the forehead before moving away again. As soon as they had disappeared I was able to open my eyes again – to an empty room!

Still Caring

Pat dropped me an e-mail to share her amazing experiences. She lives in England but thankfully her departed husband was able to find her when she went on holiday. Our loved ones in spirit find us anywhere if we need them!

Pat told me:

I felt I had to write to you about three things that have happened to me. The first is about my daughter, who was very close to her granddad. He passed away when she was three. When she was told that Granddad was not coming to see her because he was with the angels, she told us she already knew. At the time my husband and I would often hear her talking to someone in bed. When we went in to see her, she was always sitting up and when we asked her what she was doing, she said she was talking to Granddad. So it seems that Granddad had already told her himself!

The second thing that happened took place after my husband Norman passed away in 1999. He had a bad heart and had been ill for a long time and been in a lot of pain before he died. One night I was sitting on my bed when I saw him walk through the wall! I was amazed. He was smiling at me and it was clear that he was no longer in pain. He looked so happy.

A month before he passed away my husband had paid for me and my daughter to go to New York for a four-day break. A friend had come too. At the time I hadn't wanted to go, but everyone had said I should because it had always been my dream to skate in Central Park. My husband had been too ill to come with us, but I'd known that he would be with us in spirit, so in the end I had decided to make the trip.

We had a wonderful time in New York, but then I went and fell on the ice when I was skating and damaged my shoulder. I didn't do anything about it whilst we were out there because to be honest I wasn't in any pain. My daughter, being a nurse, wanted me to go to hospital, but I teased her and told her she just wanted to see the inside of a New York hospital! I didn't want it to spoil the holiday and it didn't. I did everything I wanted to.

On the way home I still wasn't in any pain but as we neared home my shoulder began to ache a little bit. I promised my daughter that when we got home I would go to hospital and get it checked out.

When I did, the hospital X-rayed my shoulder and realized there was a serious problem. I was rushed to a London hospital, where I had a five-hour operation on my shoulder. I learned later that I had shattered every bone in it and had bits of bone floating in my blood! It was very serious indeed and I ended up with 56 stitches and now have a false shoulder. How was it that I hadn't felt any pain? The surgeon told me I could have died on the plane coming home!

However, I always felt my husband was looking after me, especially as I'd seem him float through the wall. I know it wasn't a dream.

CHAPTER 4

Angels as Guardians

The guardian angels of life fly so high as to be beyond our sight, but they are always looking down upon us.

Johann Paul Richter

There have been many times when I have felt protected by angels. As a child I sensed them around me, and I have again as an adult, especially whilst driving the car. Like many people who have written to me I have heard strong warning voices and felt the promptings of my intuition, and I believe these have been communications from angels.

My own experiences are interesting, but I receive many more dramatic stories from other people. I am constantly stunned by how angels seem to help people whose lives are in danger. Some of the most amazing lifesaving experiences appear in this chapter. Remember, all of these stories are real and happened to ordinary men and women around the world.

Angels down the Mine

Susan's granddad had a lucky escape down a mine. I'll let Susan herself tell the story:

> My mum's father's family has a very strong psychic 'gene' running through it. Many of the family have had unusual psychic experiences. But Granddad was a 'tell it how it is' no-nonsense miner.

Despite his down-to-earth attitude, Susan's granddad had still experienced psychic phenomena throughout his life:

> He and my grandma lived in Upholland Moor in Lancashire in a stone semi-detached house that had at one point been a pub converted into two properties. On many, many occasions he used to see a young lady in the house and felt very frustrated when he could see her quite clearly in the room but my grandma couldn't.

Strangely, several years after her granddad had passed on, Susan said that the family discovered the old pub where they had lived had actually been called the Angel!

Susan told me more about her granddad:

> My granddad was a fireman down the pit. It was called Quaker House Colliery at Windy Arbour near Orrell and

was independently owned. Several of the miners, my granddad included, reported seeing a strange man down the mine who had a ginger-tinged beard.

None of the miners were scared of the vision, just bemused by it.

Susan continues:

It was pit policy that no one went down the mine on their own, but my granddad knew the pit and his job backwards, so one morning he did go down the pit alone.

But Granddad was not quite 'alone' that day, and thank goodness:

They were trying to break into a new seam, so he took his equipment down there and set to.

It wasn't long before he heard a voice shouting, 'John! John!' Granddad had thought he was down the mine on his own, so he went in the direction of the voice to investigate.

Granddad didn't see anyone, but his search took him away from the area in which he had been working. He had just moved away when the whole ceiling collapsed right where he had been standing!

Granddad was deeply shocked! The rocks formed such a blockage that they never managed to retrieve the cutting equipment after the fall. If Granddad had been left there, he would probably never have been found. He'd had a very lucky escape that day, and all thanks to the mystery voice, which quite literally saved his life.

As we have already discovered, Susan's granddad was no stranger to psychic phenomena. As Susan explains:

On another occasion he woke up very, very early and insisted to my grandma that he needed to get to work urgently. So she dutifully made his jam sandwiches, which he insisted were the only thing that tasted good down the mine, and he set off. When he got there two men were in trouble down the mine and he was needed to help get them out.

It's clear that Granddad had been picking up some sort of distress signal. It seems that the angel guardians were at work once again! If angels come from up above, they don't seem to mind working underground one bit!

'Don't Go to Sleep'

Tracy is from the USA. She wrote,

About five years ago I was working double shifts as a nurse at my job in Belleville, Illinois. One day I did my shift without anything unusual happening and then got home around 9 p.m. I was very tired, but I tried to stay up with the children as long as possible.

> I finally managed to crawl into bed to go to sleep. I am a very good sleeper and can usually sleep OK even with two or three children playing in the background, but on this particular night, a voice disturbed me. As I lay there it said, 'Get up, you can't go to sleep.' Well, I ignored it because I had just worked a 16-hour shift! Still it persisted. I had no idea where it was coming from, but the more I tried to get some sleep, the louder it became. I even tried telling it that I was tired and staying in bed, but it was very insistent.

Clearly 'someone' or 'something' was determined that Tracy should get out of bed:

> It felt as though something was literally pushing me out of the bed and in the end I felt I had no choice but to get up.
>
> The voice carried on and told me I had to go and buy a carbon monoxide detector. I know it sounds strange, but at no point did I feel frightened by the voice – only annoyed at being awake!

Tracy finally decided to listen and drove to the nearest store and bought a carbon monoxide detector as she had been told.

> After I had plugged it in, the counter on it immediately measured deadly levels! I was stunned. I opened all our windows and called the fire department. The children and I

were all given oxygen and the house was checked to see where the leak was.

My husband had been repairing our roof just a couple of days before and he had somehow inadvertently changed the air outlet! It's an easy mistake to make, but one with such deadly consequences. The paramedics told me we were lucky to be alive and the fire department said that our house had one of the highest levels of CO^2 they had ever seen.

Tracy never did find out who her guardian angel had been that day, but she and her family will be forever grateful.

Warning in the House

Caron is from the UK. When she wrote to me it reminded me of something I had done myself on more than one occasion. Caron recalls:

One night last month my boyfriend Mark and I were going up to bed and as I was walking up the stairs something told me to go back down and check the house. I walked around and checked that everything was switched off. I know it sounds strange, but I just had a nagging feeling that something could happen during the night.

Caron checked and unplugged everything, including the television and the DVD sockets, which she admitted only got unplugged when the family was on holiday:

> I checked the gas cooker and the fire, even though it hadn't been on, and I even unplugged the light that I leave on every night, leaving the downstairs in total darkness. (This we never do.)

I found myself nodding as I read Caron's letter. Who unplugs the TV at the wall every single night? Most of us have such large TVs that it's impossible to even get close to the socket. But Caron was picking something up and it was sensible of her to follow through on her instincts, as we all should. She continued:

> I had switched everything off, yet I still had this nagging feeling. But after spending so much time checking everything I could think of, I just didn't know what else to do. Mark asked me what I was doing and I just explained that I was checking everything had been switched off. I never told him what I was feeling, because even to me it felt a little silly.

Caron slept through the night without incident, but woke up very early the next morning.

As I walked down the stairs I stopped and started to go into what I can only explain as a daydream. I saw smoke floating up the stairs as if there had been a fire of some sort. Then I walked into the living room, which was full of smoke.

Caron was experiencing a sort of premonition:

After a crazy minute or so I snapped out of it and found myself thinking, 'What was that?' I was so confused.

Slowly I walked down the stairs. There was no smoke, no fire ... However, without thinking I walked straight over to the corner of my living room where I had left a candle lit. It was still burning from the night before!

Caron immediately realized she'd had a lucky escape, but that wasn't all:

Hanging over the candle flame was a plant. Its leaves were burnt, as it was only a couple of centimetres away from the flame. How this had not set it on fire I do not know. I could not believe what I had done.

How had the candle not set the whole house on fire? It made no sense at all. Caron says:

I ran upstairs to tell Mark, but I couldn't explain my feelings about the night before or the strange vision I'd had in the morning. Something strange was going on!

Now I firmly believe that before I went to bed the angels were trying to tell me that I had to go back to blow the candle out. Why else would I have done what I did and switched my light off in the living room? I really should have noticed the candle burning at that time, but must have been too tired. I walked through the room in total darkness and still I missed the candle!

Caron knows that angels gave her a little helping hand and averted a tragedy:

I believe angels saved our lives by stopping the candle from setting the plant on fire and then the following morning they gave me a lesson in life by showing me what had almost happened to us (me, my partner, my unborn child due in three weeks' time and my dog Lewis). It makes me shudder now just to think about it.

Now Caron knows that she is being watched over:

I can't thank the angels enough. I have had many experiences like this throughout my life and once researched the afterlife myself. Only recently a friend gave me your book *An Angel Saved my Life* and somehow it's as though it was passed to me for a reason. In the last two days I even had a white feather in my bed (although I admit, it could be from the padding!) but then last night when I was at the kitchen window a white feather fell in

> front of the window and landed on the floor. I believe it was another sign.

Caron sent me this e-mail a while ago, so I decided to contact her and see how she had been getting on. I can tell you that she safely delivered a baby girl a few weeks after she contacted me.

'Don't Fall off the Mountain'

David is from England. He was at college when his experience happened. Who would have thought that a simple college trip could have gone so wrong?

> When I left school I attended Chester College of Further Education. I took a physical education course and one year during the summer we were told we would be going to Snowdonia on a camping trip.
>
> Part of the trip would include a climb up Snowdon itself. Everyone was looking forward to the trip, although not necessarily to the long climb!
>
> When the day arrived it was lovely and sunny with hardly a cloud in the sky. We all set off eager to get to the top as we were told it was a lot more fun coming down the other side. The tutor explained that there were small loose stones called 'scree' covering the side of the mountain which allowed you to sort of 'ski' down.

The students found the trek a lot of hard work and after a short way were already exhausted. As David put it, 'About halfway up we all started getting a bit tired and moany.' The tutor cleverly told the students that there was a shop at the top of the mountain that sold cold drinks and ice cream. 'Of course nobody really believed him,' David said, 'but it egged us on all the same!'

The students pressed on and were soon at the top. David told me, 'As you can guess there was no shop when we got to the top, but the view was magnificent and worth all the effort.'

Everyone soon spotted the fun way down and couldn't wait to get going. 'We were told that if we jumped out and down, when you landed you slid quite far, so it really was like skiing.'

Everyone managed to do this and everyone went straight down except David. He'd taken one large jump that had taken him a lot further than everyone else and had skidded off to the left somehow and ended up off course and separated from the others. Before he knew what had happened, he had slipped right over a ledge.

Now David found himself clinging precariously to the mountain with a 100-foot drop below him. He was just dangling from his fingertips and no one had even noticed. He tried desperately to get a better grip, but the boulder he was hanging on to was too big and his arms were not long enough to reach.

Now this is when it gets very strange. One minute David was clinging on for dear life and the next he was standing back up on the ledge looking over it again. He has no idea how he got back up. He has no memory of it at all:

> I really thought I was going to die and was just clinging on for dear life. There is no way I could have got back on top of that boulder, I just didn't have the strength in me – but even if I had lifted myself up, why don't I remember it happening? There was no one around me to even help! One minute I was facing certain death and the next I had just been lifted to safety.
>
> Now I don't know why, but I never told anyone about it once we got to the bottom. It sounds strange now, but I just carried on as if nothing had happened. I doubt anyone would have believed me anyway!

David was shocked and bemused. He wondered for years afterwards what had happened to him on that sunny day up the mountain. He says:

> It wasn't until many years later, when I researched the subject a little, that I realized that I had been saved by my 'guardian angel'.

I know that David has had other experiences since. Perhaps I can get him to share them in the future!

A Falling Tree

This next story comes from Canada and contains many mysteries. Angels seem to have introduced another trick here, or perhaps there is a logical explanation – but I doubt it!

Julie wrote to tell me about her husband Avery's experience. Avery explained:

> I had been cutting firewood for three weeks out in the bush and this particular day was a Friday. It was beautiful in the bush with the sun shining and there was about two inches of snow on the ground.

Avery was very experienced at chopping trees, so no particular problems were expected. He carried on with his work:

> There was a big crooked oak tree that was leaning heavily. It made sense to cut it down from a safety point of view. I had it well notched and then cut from behind around both sides.

Avery admits that although he was experienced, the cutting tools he was using that day weren't really up to the task:

I was using a small saw that I knew didn't have much power for cutting such a large tree. To be honest, I was prepared to run if anything happened.

Happen it did. All of a sudden the tree began to fall. It broke off quickly and made such a noise it sounded like a rifle shot. Avery was ready to run as he had planned, but something went terribly wrong:

It was as if I was frozen to the spot! I was just unable to move for about five whole seconds. It seemed as if all the clouds in the sky had come down to the ground – everything was white. I could no longer see any trees at all and the whole bush was filled with nothing but white clouds.

Avery got his bearings and found himself well away from the path of the tree behind some rocks. It made no sense, because the tree had been falling in his direction:

It was as if someone from above caught me and threw me over the rock ledge. I do not know how the wind was knocked out of me, but when I came to, my chain saw was still idling about eight feet away and I was lying in a hole beside a rock that I hadn't even seen before.

Like so many other people who have similar experiences, Avery was totally confused as to what had just happened to him. One minute he was paralysed in the path of a falling tree, the next he was safely behind some rocks which seemed to have kept him from getting hit by the tree. He just couldn't make it out at all:

> I went to my truck and brought my measuring tape to measure from where my last step was (when I saw all the white clouds) to where I ended up under the rock ledge and it was 16 feet away! I had travelled 16 feet through trees with nothing broken. In fact the only sign that anything had happened at all was a small scratch on my knee. I had no pain anywhere!

In actual fact the tree *had* fallen on him, but it had landed on the rocks, which had kept it safely off his body. Avery went back to his truck shaking and praying:

> I had never been so scared in my whole life. This tree had landed on top of me but I had been lying below the rock ledge so it had never touched me and the barbered piece was on the other side of me. If I had been allowed to run the way I had planned, I would have been killed instantly because that was the way the tree fell ... and landed.

After about 15 minutes Avery went back to the place he had been thrown from:

> Something was not right. There were no marks in the snow and if you were to look at where I had been standing and where I ended up (16 feet away, remember), you would know I simply couldn't have jumped that far. The only marks were when I went to get up. I had left my knee and hand marks in the snow at that point.

Avery did have a few thoughts on the experience:

> My best friend who worked in the bush for me off and on for many years was killed three years ago when a tree landed on him. He had been working by himself and was not found for two days. On Christmas Day I had been to visit his grave site. Before I got to the graveyard I saw around 12 white birds flying around. They were as white as the snow – as white as the white clouds I saw that day. That was the first time I had ever seen white birds in this area. They were smaller than chickadees and swarmed around my van like bees would swarm around a person for a whole minute.

Had Avery's deceased friend been his guardian angel?

> When I got back home I continued reading a book my sister had given me. It contained stories about incidents like this and said that a sign such as seeing white birds could well mean that someone had saved my life that day, although I only read about this after I came home.

Avery knows for sure that someone or something intervened that day. 'It is said that everyone has a guardian angel and that day I found mine.'

Was It a Ghost?

Wendy, from Hull, was just a young girl when she had her unusual encounter, but she's never forgotten her ghostly angel:

> When I was about nine months old we moved house to a bungalow in a nearby village with my parents and my three-year-old brother Peter. When I was three Mum and Dad had our bungalow turned into a dormer so that we could have two bedrooms upstairs, one mine, the other Peter's. This was the first time we'd had stairs.

Wendy was unfamiliar with the dangers that a staircase offered and was not as careful as she should have been – but then three year olds are easily distracted anyway!

> Not long afterwards the rooms were completed and I was excited to have my own room at last. Then one day I was struggling with my dolls' wooden cot. I clearly remember I was dragging it across the landing when it got stuck in the carpet. Of course, silly me was walking backwards and pulling the cot backwards in the direction of the stairs.

It's easy to see now how Wendy's situation was precarious. It's like watching one of those scary films when you wonder how the victim can't see what's just about to happen! Wendy told me:

> The stairs were varnished and I was wearing socks. Being very small, I just couldn't see the danger and fell backwards. Rather bizarrely, I left the top step in a sitting position, although I don't know how that happened. I remember 'falling' down the stairs and as I did so I stroked my hand along the wallpaper all the way down. I seemed to float along and didn't hit one step on the way down. I landed at the bottom completely safely and as I stood up I looked up at the cot on the landing – it was half off and half on the top step.

She'd had a very lucky escape!

Wendy might only have been three, but even at that young age she remembered the details of the incident clearly:

> Peter was at school and my dad was at work. Mum was in the kitchen, so there was no one around who could have 'lifted' me in any way. I wondered about it for years afterwards.

Then, three years later, another strange thing happened. Could this have involved the same unseen helper? Wendy told me:

> When I was six, one winter's night I was playing with my toys on the floor of Peter's room. I remember that Peter was on his bed, my dad had gone out for a drink and my mum was taking a bath. My brother stood up and said he was going downstairs, so I carried on playing for a bit and quickly became bored. I remember moving across to the doorway and as I looked into my bedroom I saw a little girl staring at me. She was very pale and she looked dark around the eyes. She wore a tartan skirt with a white vest attached but had nothing on her legs or feet.

Wendy was bewildered as to how this little girl had got into the house, but wanted her to feel welcome:

> I walked past her into my bedroom and sat down, folding my legs, and she did the same but she never said a word, she just stared, looking really sad. I decided to sing her a song to cheer her up. Before I finished the end of the song I reached out to hold her hand and I remember feeling shocked that her hands were so cold. At that point I seemed to startle her and she stood up and moved to the top of the stairs. As she took her first step she drifted down the stairs, gathering speed as she went. Her body echoed as she went and then vanished through the wall at the bottom. I remember feeling scared, knowing that this was not normal, but I didn't know what a ghost was at that age.

Who was this little girl? Wendy always wondered. Over the years she talked about her strange experiences to her family and friends and anyone who would listen, but she never felt happy with any of the explanations given to her. Then, about ten years ago, she felt she finally had her answer:

> Mum and Dad had called around to pick up my son. I had to be at work, but was in a bit of a panic because my hairdryer wasn't working properly. Mum looked concerned and said to Dad, 'Oh, Jeff, cut the plug off that thing. You remember what happened to that little girl in Bilton.'
>
> Straightaway it took me back to that little girl and I asked again what had happened when I was younger. I challenged my parents over it, saying, 'But you said you didn't know of any girl passing away ...?'
>
> Mum and Dad exchanged glances and realized I was now plenty old enough to know the truth.
>
> 'Apparently, a little girl was staying with her grandparents a few bungalows down from us,' Mum said. 'She died when she was electrocuted by her grandmother's hairdryer. You were a baby when it happened and I used to feel awful passing their house with you in the pram and Peter beside me. We moved away shortly afterwards.'

Wendy wondered whether that young girl had been the one who had saved her when she had fallen down the stairs. She says, 'Wherever she is now, I hope she is at peace.'

Strange Delays

Lee's story is an interesting one. Although at first there seems no mystery involved, when you put all the facts together, it's clear that something 'lucky' happened here. She explained:

> When I was 21 years old I was living with my dad. I had a four-month-old son called Jordan and he was living with us too. My mum had left when I was just 13 years old and Dad had never really got over it. Bless him, he had become a heavy drinker since she'd left.

Lee and her dad were very close and her father loved his little grandson Jordan. Lee told me:

> One ordinary night I went to bed as usual. I had planned an early start the following morning. I wanted to visit my ex-boyfriend's parents and take over their grandson for a visit.
>
> That night I had a dream that every time I went to go out of the door to visit my friends I had forgotten something. I had to keep going back for it. This happened over and over again. It was either the baby's bottles or nappies or my keys. The list was endless. By the time I had collected everything together it was too late to go anywhere.

Lee woke up feeling cross and frustrated by her dream and was surprised to see a visitor in her room:

At the end of the bed where my son's cradle stood there was a figure hovering in the air and it was glowing white – and very large. I had no idea why it was there, but I immediately felt at peace and wasn't frightened at all. It stayed for a few seconds then went away, so I drifted right back to sleep.

The next morning I was up bright and early and went downstairs to get the baby's bottle ready for him. As I went into the living room, my dad was lying on the floor with a cigarette in his hand. I asked him why he was lying on the floor and he said he had a terrible pain in his head. I immediately jumped into action and took the cigarette off him, at the same time telling him to go and lie upstairs in his bedroom.

Shortly afterwards, when I went upstairs, Dad was just coming out of the bathroom. He looked odd to me and it was clear that something wasn't quite right.

Lee's dad had just had a stroke, and the following drama meant that she didn't make her trip, just as the dream had predicted.

Her dad was ill for a long time after that. Lee says:

It wasn't until a little while after it all happened that I remembered the dream and the figure at the end of the bed. I now

> know it was an angel sent to guide and support me and keep me strong while my dad was ill.

Lee had her dad for another four years after that and she feels that it was all thanks to her angel. 'I still really miss him,' she says, 'and I know that if it wasn't for that angel I wouldn't have coped as well as I did.'

She is 35 now and has gone on to have a daughter as well. She knows that her dad and her angel are keeping an eye on her two beautiful children.

A Near Miss

Here is a quick story for you from Karen. She told me:

> When I heard that angels need to be invited into our lives, I decided to talk to mine. I told them that I was sorry I'd not acknowledged them before and that they were welcome in my life and asked them to give me a sign that they were there.

Karen wasn't too sure what sort of sign she was looking for, but had a good laugh when it came:

> Immediately after asking I went upstairs to sort my ten-year-old daughter's sock drawer (what lovely jobs us mums have!) The first pair of socks I picked up were old ones that my daughter had never worn. To be honest I could hardly

remember them, but lo and behold there on the side were the words 'Little Angel' and a picture of an angel! I know it was my sign. I am sure of it.

Even so, it was hardly a dramatic sign, but shortly afterwards Karen feels she had a little help from the angels:

A week after this I was out running with my friend and was jogging slightly in front of her. I came to the junction of a busy road and stood waiting to cross for a few seconds. For some reason, and with no conscious decision, I turned round and started jogging back to meet my friend. At that very moment, a very large HGV lorry mounted the pavement exactly where I had been standing. I was totally shocked. If I'd stayed in that spot just a fraction of a second longer, I could easily have been under the wheels of the lorry.

Luckily she was fine and Karen feels that maybe her new angel friends had more than a little to do with it!

An Angel Guardian on the Phone

Here is another short story for you. This lady asked not to be identified but gave permission for her story to be included here. She told me:

I have been aware of my two guardian angels around me for many years and have often spoken to them. I am only now becoming more open to their presence, but despite this I think there have been several instances in the past when they have helped me. One particularly stands out in my mind.

About two-and-a-half years ago, I was alone in the house at about 10 p.m. My husband's work at the time meant he was on a night shift. I had been having a difficult time personally and was feeling depressed. Just then, a member of my family phoned. This family member has some issues of his own and was drunk and aggressive. He said threatening things about my husband and suggested that he and I should have a relationship.

Not being in the best frame of mind, I was really scared and I asked my guardian angel to help me. Then I felt that I was holding my angel's hand, which I could feel very solidly, and that he was reassuring me.

His presence made me feel loved and supported, but I was still nervous. Squeezing my hand, my angel said, 'Everything is going to be fine.'

At that moment, my aggressive caller said, 'Who's that? Who's there with you? I just heard a man's voice!' Then he quickly made an excuse and hung up!

It seems as though this lovely lady had the confirmation that she needed. Angels do have a voice if they want one!

'Everything is Going to Be Fine'

Here is another story that is very similar to the last one. This lady explained:

> I was feeling very low the other night due to a few things that have happened in my life recently, so I decided to say a prayer to my angels. I just asked them to protect me and to watch over one of my family members who had been very ill.
>
> As I started to go to sleep that night I thought that someone had turned the light on in my room. As I opened my eyes I could see a very bright white light in front of me, just above my chest. I could also see what appeared to be a twisting spiral of mist or smoke right in the middle of the light. It was really comforting and as I watched it I felt overcome with happiness and joy. I heard a soft voice say, 'Everything is going to be fine.' Then the light faded away and I was left lying in the dark feeling extremely happy.
>
> Since I had this experience my family member is a lot better and things have been going really well for me in my life.

Isn't it strange how the angelic phrase in these two experiences was the same?

'One of My Four Angels'

OK, go on then, here's another one! Joyce is from England and her story, although different from the others, has that same phrase again. I'll let Joyce tell it herself:

> I have only recently become aware that some people believe in angels, although as a child I used the old prayer 'Four corners to my bed, four angels round my bed ...' I considered this belief to be childhood comfort and nothing more, but reading your column and the letters readers have written reminded me of an incident that happened some years ago. It was such an intense experience that I did wonder what it meant.
>
> I had just broken off my engagement to a young man that I thought I loved. The reasons for the break-up were very distressing and left me feeling humiliated and depressed. Never having had much self-esteem, I thought I would never find anyone else who would love me the way I longed to be loved.
>
> One night I went to bed and cried myself to sleep yet again. However, that night I had a very vivid dream. I was walking along a path close to my ex-fiancé's home when I saw him in the garden and began to turn away. He saw me and called my name and then he began to come towards me, but the thought of speaking to him frightened me. I ran away from him down a small path between two houses.

Suddenly, I ran headlong into another 'man'. I looked up, but I couldn't see his face because it seemed to be covered with something (a sort of mist or a veil, I think). The man put his arms around me and held me firmly yet gently. Right away a feeling of warm contentment washed over me and he said, 'It's going to be alright.' Then I woke up!

The feeling of contentment and well-being lasted for most of the following day and I never felt quite so sad again. A few years later I did meet another man and this one turned out to be very special. We married and have been together ever since (nearly 23 years next autumn).

I don't know what all this meant. Was it one of my 'four angels' or was I just desperate to be reassured? Whatever the explanation, it certainly turned out to be a special event in my life and I have never forgotten it.

Protection on a Bike

Ine is from Belgium and was a young girl when she had a very frightening experience. It's amazing how these encounters stick in our minds, isn't it?

Ine explained:

I used to ride my bike home from school alone and always carried my very heavy schoolbag on the back of it. Near to my home there is a small forest. All the trees stand very close to each other and in the middle of the forest there is a small and dusty road.

One day when I was 16 years old, I had just ridden into this forest when something scared me. Initially I thought that someone very pale was standing there but then assumed I must have seen a white painted circle on the trees, the kind they use to mark a tree that needs cutting down. Anyway, it scared me so much that I started to cycle faster, though when I passed the dusty road I felt a bit silly and started to slow down again.

It was then that Ine heard somebody calling out to her:

A man was approaching me and asking me to wait. I thought he wanted to ask for directions. He looked a bit tired as he tried to catch up with me, but when he got closer he started to pull at my bike. He was trying to push me off the road and into the field! After my fright a few moments before, I still had such an adrenaline rush that I was strong enough to fight him off. I rode as fast as I could back home.

Ine's mother immediately rang the police, because her little sister was still behind her on the road and they were very worried that this madman was still around. 'My dad is a policeman and he arrived very quickly,' Ine told me, 'but luckily my sister was already home. She had seen the man and he was already waiting for his next victim on the dusty road in the forest.'

When Ine's father and his colleague arrived at the scene they saw Ine's sister's friend riding very fast and crying. 'He'd got to her too and she had screamed so hard she could hardly speak anymore.'

Sadly the crazy man was never caught, but Ine wonders whether she would have been alert enough to escape him if she hadn't already been frightened by the white shape in the forest:

> My friendly nature would almost certainly have meant that I would have stopped to help this guy. Chances are, there would have been a whole different outcome for me.

Ine told the story to her boyfriend and a few days later the two of them rode back to the same spot to see if they could find any white markings on the trees, but they never found anything.

She feels that she had a guardian angel: 'I like to think something in that forest was protecting me.'

Another 'Bike Angel'

Strangely, a few days after I received Ine's bike-angel story I received a similar story. This one came from Denise in England. She wrote:

> I had an experience 30 years ago and it has stayed with me ever since. I was actually walking home from a night out at the time and was pushing my bike rather than riding it. Then I was approached by this man who threw my bike

onto the road and started to attack me! He just came from nowhere! It was 11.30 at night and there was no one around. I was just terrified and I honestly thought he was going to rape me or even kill me. I struggled and tried to scream.

After a moment Denise and her attacker realized they were not alone:

I turned and spotted a middle-aged woman dressed in a white suit with short black hair. My attacker had also seen something, because he immediately let go of me and ran for his life – the way you might have done if you had seen the devil! Maybe he didn't see the same thing as me. I often wondered!

The lady was amazing. She asked me if I was OK and then walked me to my mother-in-law's house, which was just a few streets away. When we arrived I turned to knock on the door and when I turned back around, the woman had simply disappeared.

Denise never forgot her saviour: 'Thirty years later I still think about that special woman who might just have saved my life that night!'

Caught!

Gabriela always remembers the angel who protected her as a young girl. This story is from Australia:

I was about 15 years old and on my way to the local outdoor swimming pool. For this reason I was dressed in a short sarong skirt and a bikini top with a singlet. Maybe my outfit was part of the problem, but as I walked on the right-hand side of the footpath a car drove past me and slowed down. As it got closer to me I looked over and felt a sort of jolt in my body. The car kept on moving forward, but something told me to cross the road. As I did this, the car turned back into my street and I started to worry. I tried to keep walking calmly, but this time as the car passed me a voice in my mind told me very strongly, 'Get the number plate, remember it, memorize it, get the number plate,' over and over again.

The car went round again and the next time it pulled over just ahead of me and as I passed the driver called out to me. I looked at him and said, 'Sorry I can't help you,' and I bravely kept walking.

He was persistent and yelled out, 'Please, I'm lost. Just show me where to go on this map.'

I looked back over at the car and realized he was behaving indecently. Then I just ran into the nearest shop. I asked the man in the shop to ring the police, but he was rude and wouldn't help me.

I was scared to leave, but in the end I felt I had no option. The man had gone, so I carried on to the pool and asked to use the phone there.

In the end I made a statement to the police and gave them the number plate I'd been told to remember. The police were very shocked that I had remembered and could not understand what had compelled me to do so.

It turned out that the man was found and arrested and charged. Apparently they had been after him for a long time. He'd been parking at schools and harassing a lot of young girls, and in their fright none of them had even managed to remember the colour of the car.

To this day I think back and remember how strongly I heard the warning that day. I don't know if I classify it as my sixth sense or angels. But I have learned to trust my instincts a lot more now and will never forget how they helped me and many other girls out there.

Butterfly Reassurance and an Ice Fall

Dorothy is from Virginia and I want to share both of her family stories with you here. It's her 'PS' story that changes this account from one of comfort to one of the miraculous!

When she was a child, Dorothy got a case of German measles:

> I was nine years old and at first I was congratulating myself on having a three-day disease that would keep me out of school. Little did I know what was in store for me!

Dorothy's simple childhood sickness developed into a life-threatening illness and she had to be rushed to hospital:

> I was bleeding internally, which was petrifying. The disease had triggered a rare side-effect that completely wiped out all my immunity and clotting factors. I literally bled to death and had to be resuscitated on several occasions. At one point I was clinically dead for over three minutes.

Life changed completely for Dorothy from that moment on:

> With no platelets my blood would not clot. I had to live in total isolation and they told me that even a common cold could kill me. For a very long time I saw only my mother and grandparents, in whose home I lived, because I could not live with a small brother and sister who would carry germs.

This sounds very difficult, but young children can adapt very well, as Dorothy explained:

Oddly, I didn't think the existence was lonely so much as boring. My strait-laced grandmother was my only playmate. I was beginning to despair that this would be my life forever. Later I was able to go for rides in the car, although I was never able to get out. But it was just such a relief to leave the house at all.

Dorothy's life seemed destined to be lived from afar, but things were to change:

One day I was in the back of the car, waiting for my mother to come out of a shop. I was feeling somewhat doomed to lead a very boring existence and I remember saying out loud, 'Please send me a sign that this is not all there is.'

At that moment, a large Monarch butterfly flew in the window of the car and landed on my lap. I was overwhelmed by the sense that everything would be OK if I could be as patient as this seemingly fearless butterfly perched on my knee.

That moment was one that changed the young girl's life from one of despair to hope. And that wasn't all that changed:

A few weeks later my weekly blood test showed growth of white cells and platelets and from then on, week after week they got better and better until I was finally able to move back home. A few months after that I was able to go back to school again.

Dorothy always felt that the butterfly was a special gift of faith:

I have always known that butterfly was an angel messenger and I have never forgotten it, even after 40 years, but I have never told anyone about it before. I always felt that nobody would understand the significance of the butterfly. So you can imagine my amazement at seeing the butterfly story on your website and realizing that similar things had happened to other people.

This story was already a special one, but then Dorothy sent me another magical family story:

It turned out I wasn't the only one in the family to have had a strange experience. One night my mother woke up in a cold sweat with a horrible feeling of dread about my brother. She had heard him calling her and had jumped out of bed and started to walk down the hall before she had realized that he wasn't calling from his bedroom. He was wintering over in the Antarctic, and was many miles from home.

My mother is an extremely strong-willed and mentally rock-stable person, so this experience really upset her. She tried to chalk it up to a bad dream, but just couldn't shake the fear.

You may have read accounts like this before where loved ones – living loved ones – seem able to communicate with each other even though their physical bodies are many miles apart. Dorothy and her family soon discovered the horrifying reason behind the 'bad dream':

> The next day, my brother managed to get a radio message to us. It seems he had been working on the ice pack when suddenly a crevasse had opened beneath him. He told us that he had started to fall and had just managed to grab hold of the ice edge. Falling into the crevice would have been certain death. He recalls screaming out, 'Mom!' as he frantically clawed his way back up the ledge, and he had actually felt a connection in a way he couldn't explain.
>
> We later worked out that Mum had woken at the exact moment that my brother had called out!
>
> Nothing like that has ever happened before or since and the episode really shook the family, but it also gave all of us knowledge that there are things in this life we just don't understand.

Of course she is right, which is why we need to keep an open mind about these things. Life does not run along in a perfectly explainable way. Not everything that happens is logical or even sensible, but one thing is for certain: amazing things still happen whether you believe in them or not!

CHAPTER 5

Angels and Children

See that you do not despise one of these little ones,
for I say to you that their angels in heaven continually see
the face of my Father who is in heaven.

Matthew 13:10

As a young girl I had my own lifesaving angel experience when I was saved from drowning off the Isle of Wight, just off the south coast of England. So I know for sure that angels do watch over children.

My own daughter saw a 'fairy man' on the ceiling of our living room after the funeral of her great grandmother, even though she hadn't attended and was way too young to have any understanding of what 'dead' meant or what an 'angel' was. A 'fairy man' was the closest description she could give with her limited vocabulary.

Though they can't always express exactly what they've seen, young children are far more open to angelic phenomena than adults are. They often see their deceased relatives and their guardian angels and even spirit children. We might dismiss such things as 'invisible friends' or even 'imaginary friends', but most children will tell you that their experiences are real and if we were only to listen to them we could learn so much.

Lots of children write and tell me about their experiences, and so do adults who had experiences as children. Here are some of them. It's strange that the first one took place on the Isle of Wight too! Just a 'coincidence', I'm sure!

Three Feathers

Sharron was just four years old and very excited. She was sitting in the back of her parents' car wearing a most beautiful dress. Along with her mum and dad, she was on the way to her uncle's wedding reception. She had been a bridesmaid at the wedding earlier in the day – a big honour for such a little girl!

The family lived on the Isle of Wight, near a place called Black Gang Chine. At that time people rarely wore seatbelts, especially on this small island; in fact many cars didn't even have them in the back at all. On this fateful day Sharron was swinging her legs backwards and forwards and admiring her beautiful new cream shoes and was not safely strapped into the vehicle. She was also playing with the door handle, something mothers everywhere tell their children not to do. It was an accident waiting to happen.

As Sharron played with the handle, the door flew open and Sharron was sucked out of the car. It was every parent's worst nightmare. The young girl had fallen right into the path of the cars behind.

As the incident occurred so quickly, Sharron's parents didn't immediately realize what had happened and continued to speed off into the distance. It was not until her mother turned round that she was even aware that her precious daughter had fallen from the car.

The next few moments were a blur of utter horror. Sharron's mother was able to see her daughter in the middle of the road behind them with vehicles rushing towards her. She screamed out to her husband and immediately he began to reverse the car back to where Sharron was lying. Were they already too late? Was their only daughter fatally injured or already dead? The next few minutes seemed to move in slow motion as the drama unfolded like a bad dream – but this was real.

Sharron's parents rushed from the car, terrified of what they might find. The young mother was crying as she removed her daughter's bonnet and kissed her gently, all the while stroking her hair over and over and chiding herself, 'If only we had checked the door ...'

But Sharron was alive. She looked up at her mother and said, 'Where did the lady go?'

The couple had seen no one and assumed that their daughter was delirious. No one was by the side of the road, after all. Relieved that their daughter was alive, the traumatized parents carefully lifted her back into the car before rushing her to the nearest hospital. The moment of confusion passed.

The couple were still shaking with fear and shock as doctors performed a series of tests on Sharron. After checking her all over, one of the doctors lifted her up onto a large hospital bed and as he did so, three white fluffy feathers fell onto the floor. The young girl was fascinated by these 'whiter than white' feathers that seemed to come from under her dress, but no one else seemed to notice them …

Amazingly, she only needed three stitches to her knee. The doctors were stunned that she had survived at all. How had a four-year-old girl fallen from a fast-moving vehicle and survived with little more than a cut on her leg?

To this day Sharron's parents firmly believe that their daughter was saved by her layered bridesmaid's dress, but she has another story and recalls trying to explain it all to the doctors and her parents at the time. None of them were interested in her explanation, but she does remember that as she left the hospital a different doctor appeared. He winked at her and said in a whisper, 'One day they will listen. Don't give up or forget today …' Then he scuffed up her hair before saying goodbye. Why did this doctor seem aware that something magical had happened but the others did not?

Sharron is now married and a mother of four children herself, but she still remembers her experience in great detail. She says that she knew that she wasn't allowed to mess around with the door handle but was still stunned when the door actually opened. She has no memory of hitting the road, but recalls a strange feeling of being 'light and fluffy'. She says that although it sounds strange, she felt as if she had fallen onto a road made of cotton wool! She felt safe during the whole incident and the only thing that upset her at the time was the fact that her mum and dad appeared to be driving away without her. She says that she was too young to know anything about angels, but clearly recalls a lady with a stunning face placing her very soft hands around her with a hug like 'a warm fluffy towel'. This beautiful lady was surrounded by the very strong smell of flowers. She sat with Sharron until her parents arrived to take over.

Sharron says that although she felt no pain, she had actually landed in the middle of the road before being guided to the side by this special lady, who had appeared just in time to ensure that she did not get killed by the traffic.

By the time Sharron's parents arrived at the scene the mysterious woman had disappeared and no one else seemed aware of the lifesaving role that she had performed.

Sharron recalls desperately trying to explain all this to both her parents and the doctors, but feels that those around her were too distracted by the trauma of the accident to listen to her explanation. Even though a doctor had said in passing, 'The angels are looking after her today,' no one had taken the comment too seriously.

However, Sharron knows the truth about what happened on that special day so many years ago – and she still has the feathers in a 'secret box' at home.

'An Angel Held Me in Her Arms'

By a strange 'coincidence', here is a very similar story. Diane wrote with the startling revelation, 'My earliest memory is of a car wheel coming towards my head …'

Diane had been involved in a serious accident. Just like Sharon she had fallen out of the back door of a car:

> The next thing I saw was the back of my mother's head. There was a man with a hat and coat driving our car and I was lying on a pillow on my mommy's lap. It didn't occur to me for years that I was seeing all of this from the back seat of the car. I remember that Mommy was crying and I wanted to make her stop. But I seemed to move away to another place.

Diane found herself being lifted out of her body and taken into the arms of an angel-type figure who cradled her, removing her from the trauma of the incident:

> A beautiful lady was holding me in her arms, cooing to me. I don't remember much about her features, but the colours I saw were gold, white and blue.
>
> I had been very scared when I saw Mommy crying, and the woman told me not to be afraid and that everything would be fine. I stayed with her, cradled in her arms, for what seemed like a long time.

Diane remembers very little about the accident after that, but says that throughout her childhood there were times when she felt the need to escape what was going on around her. At such times:

> I would go to this lady and she would make it better. It's as though she's always been there for me. I don't need it so much anymore, but sometimes I find her there anyway, just to give me a hug.

Over the years her mother filled in the lost details of her childhood accident:

> We lived in Des Moines, the capital city of Iowa. Mother was driving the car with my three sisters and me in the back seat. At the time we were aged one through three. I have a

twin and we were two at the time. Mom said that we were playing sort of roughly and the back door flew open and I fell out.

Diane suffered a cracked skull. She had no hair left after the accident and had to have 26 stitches. As an adult she began having panic attacks and experienced terrible pain all over her body:

I felt as if my skin was being burned off me. I went to see a counsellor and she recommended I get more information on this accident.

Sadly by this time my mom had died, but Dad was very helpful. He told me, 'Well, you know, I was working and not able to get to the hospital until late, but at 10.30 at night a nice nurse showed me to your room. There you were in that crib with tubes everywhere. You looked like a meatball.'

Diane was shocked by this and had no idea what he meant until her father explained:

He told me I'd had every ounce of flesh scraped from my body when I rolled on the pavement. As soon as I heard that, the pain in my body went away and I've never had another panic attack since.

No wonder Diane had been lifted from her body. I imagine the pain would have been unbearable for such a small girl. But Diane had her angel lady and, unlike many children, she retained this contact well into adulthood.

The Children on the Bus

When Ian drove to work one morning he took more than his packed lunch along for the ride. Angels were ahead of him on the road, ready to ensure that everyone arrived at their destination in one piece.

This experience happened over 30 years ago, but Ian told me that it was still very clear in his mind, even after all this time. He explained:

> I used to work for a major bank and at the time it was their policy to send the new clerks, particularly men, out of their comfort zone and make them go to places well away from their abodes.

I could sympathize. My own husband worked for a major bank at that time and he too was sent to a new branch many miles away from home. I knew that if Ian wanted to progress in his career he would have to be prepared to move around the country. It's just the way it worked in those days.

Ian lived in Liverpool and was sent to work in North Wales, in Shotton. Packing a suitcase and a few belongings, he found the digs that had been arranged for him. They were in Hawarden, about three miles away from his work and up a very steep hill.

He made the journey to the bank every single day and soon got used to it. In fact, he told me, he made the trip so often that he became blasé about it:

> From Hawarden the road dropped steeply between a cemetery built into a hill on one side and a high wall which, if I remember correctly, hid quite tall buildings. The road was steep and had a number of sharp bends, but most vehicles would travel at, or a little in excess of, the speed limit.

We can all be a little careless when we follow a regular routine and it's sometimes hard to remember that disaster can be just moments away if we take our attention from the road. Ian had a shock:

> On this particular morning I was at the head of a line of vehicles and on my own, *physically*, in my car. When I approached the next to last bend, I heard a man's voice loudly telling me to slow down as if I did not, I would drive into a bus full of children who were crossing the road right ahead of me.

Ian was stunned by the mystery voice, but even as he pondered it his body was automatically reacting:

> I was sceptical at the time, but the shock caused me to place my foot on the brake, much to the annoyance of the motorists behind, I might say. Some of them started to flash their lights at me or blow their horns, so you can imagine the speed of my reaction. It hadn't been expected by the other drivers.

As Ian turned that final bend he shook his head in amazement:

> Imagine the shock and feelings of great fright when, on rounding the last bend, I found a coach full of schoolchildren directly in front of my car. I know that although there was a short distance to travel to the bus, if I had not been told so clearly by the voice, I could never have stopped in time. As well as killing some, or all, of the children, I would probably have lost my own life too.

As Ian admitted, he had completely forgotten that there was a crossing on that part of the road. He knows the voice saved many people from great tragedy that day.

> Whenever I think of this, and I do often, I thank my guardian angel for saving the lives of the children and, of course, my own. You know, at the time of this event I was not remotely interested in the spirit or angelic realms, although now I am a working medium and have been able to help a number of people with proof of life eternal.

So Ian's life was changed forever after his angel spoke to him that day on the road.

There's Something about Jayda

There was always something about Jayda. Even from a young age, her family could sense that this little one was different from other children.

Jayda's mum, Michelle, is from London. She told me:

> When Jayda was 12 months old she wouldn't go to bed unless she was wearing her socks because 'the man' tickled her feet when she was sleeping and she didn't like it. Then when she was two years old she complained that the man was scaring her, which was a little more worrying. There were plenty of other experiences until one night I heard her talking and laughing (I must admit it gave me the shivers). I went into her bedroom to ask her what she was laughing at and she told me that there was an angel under her bed hiding from me and that he had been pulling funny faces to make her laugh!

As Jayda got older, her ability to see and hear spirit energies just grew. Her mother explained:

> I have always believed in angels and spirits and have also seen and heard spirits, although I do try to shut it out because I still get scared, but when Jayda told me there was

an angel in her room I just assumed she had an imaginary friend. However, Jayda's angel turned out to be quite genuine. She spoke about him every day.

Jayda appeared to be communicating with the highest energies of all. Michelle said:

One day I asked her about her angel and she told me his name was Michael, and that he was her 'brother'!

Michelle remembers a strange experience connected to Michael:

We were all sitting in the living room and the younger ones were watching a children's programme on the television when Jayda started talking about Michael again. She kept going to the back of the television to talk to him. I have to say, at the time I didn't really pay much attention to it.

That day I had been taking a lot of photographs of the children and when I went to get them developed I was a little freaked by what I saw! Whenever Jayda had been talking to Michael, there was an unexplained flash of light or shape in the photograph.

The photograph of the television was the strangest of all:

There was the face of a boy coming through the screen! After that I took more of an interest in Jayda's angel and found it quite reassuring that she was being watched over. Sadly, when we moved home Jayda told me that Michael was unable to come with us.

I've never spoken to Jayda since about her angel friend, but I still have the unpacked box of photographs somewhere!

'My Daughter Sees Angels'

Jenni sent me an e-mail from her home in Finland:

> One day I asked my five-year-old girl if she had ever seen an angel. I truly expected to get a 'no' as her answer and I felt silly even asking, but to my surprise she said, 'Yes!' right away.

It's amazing how children keep these things from us. Perhaps it's worth asking your own children just in case! Jenni was stunned when her daughter began telling her about the day she saw an angel:

> She reminded me of a day when the family had visited a zoo. At the time she had been four years old. She could remember my mother being with us and her little brother being asleep in the pram. She told me an angel appeared at her side when we were looking at the rabbits! She said the angel was a girl about her age with blonde hair and wings. The angel child smiled at her, stayed by her side

> for a while and then flew up in the air and circled behind her.

Jenni couldn't believe what she was hearing, especially all the detail in the story, but:

> When I thought about it, it made sense. I remembered the whole situation just as she had explained it (it wasn't so long ago). I remembered standing behind my daughter and looking at her and she was obviously very surprised, even startled, by something she had seen to the right. I thought she had spotted another animal and asked her, 'What's the matter, honey? What are you looking at?' And she didn't utter a word.

Now Jenni wanted to know more:

> I decided to ask her why she hadn't told me about the experience at the time and she said that she thought it was a secret, because no one else had seen the angel. She also explained that she hadn't talked about seeing the angel afterwards because no one had asked her about it!

If you ask your own children, you might well get a similar reply.

After that Jenni decided it was worth questioning her daughter a little more. The little girl explained that although the day at the zoo had been her first experience of an angel, she had seen them many times since:

> She told me how an angel had appeared to her when she had been playing alone in the sandbox in our back yard. She called this the 'mother angel', which I understand meant that the angel had appeared as a woman.
>
> Then she told me about a time when she had seen an angel while she had been running around with her friends in the playground in front of our house. At the time she told her friends, although I'm not sure they believed her.
>
> On another occasion she had seen an angel standing behind our neighbour's boy (a six-year-old) in the playground and she had told him, too, but he hadn't been able to see anything.

There were so many experiences here it was as if Jenni had opened a magical box and her daughter had set her experiences free:

> She also told me that an angel had gone through our window once.
>
> Then one day last week we went shopping and bought her a sleigh. She wanted to stay outside and play with it in the snow whilst I put her little brother to bed. She was so excited about playing outside and after a couple of minutes she had put on her winter clothes and even her winter boots. Then she jumped right next to me and I was

quite irritated about it at first, but then she told me that she had got scared because she had thought she had seen a ghost! It had been an angel again, but this time it had had multi-coloured hair.

Jenni was kind enough to say that learning about angels through reading one of my books had helped to open up her relationship with her daughter:

It has really enriched the relationship between my daughter and me and she feels now that she can tell me all about her experiences.

Not everyone in the family is a believer, though. Jenni says:

My husband is a real sceptic and does not want to discuss angels at all. But I really do believe my daughter sees angels. I don't doubt it. She would never ever make up anything like that. We are so close, I know she speaks the truth.

So you see, you never know what you might find out if you just ask!

Happy Christmas, Cherry!

How much do our little ones see that we don't? Plenty, by the sounds of this next story. Denise is from Cardiff in Wales and she wrote to tell me about her four-year-old niece Katie:

> Katie goes to nursery and at Christmastime last year her mum was writing Christmas cards out for friends in nursery when Katie kept insisting she write a card for someone called Cherry. Her mother had no idea who Cherry was, but Katie was so determined that eventually she went ahead and wrote a card for Cherry, even though she knew that there was no one in the class with that name.

This was when things took a strange turn, as Denise explains:

> When I took the Christmas cards into the school the following day I asked the teacher if there was anyone by the name of Cherry in the class. The teacher said no, but Katie was adamant that there was.

Had Katie seen someone in the class that no one else could see? Denise explains:

> At the end of nursery that day, Katie's teacher asked if she could have a quiet word with me. She explained that she'd

asked around the nursery to see if anybody knew a person named Cherry and one of the teachers said there had been a lady named Cherry who used to clean the nursery, but she had passed away many years ago!

It seems that Cherry, who had really loved her work, was still very much a part of the nursery school all those years later, even if Katie had been the only one to see her – that we know of!

Childhood Visions

Sarah contacted me from Scotland. She believes that children are far more receptive to spirits because they have not yet convinced themselves that certain things do not exist. I'm sure she's right!

Sarah was a psychic child herself. She says:

> As we get older, we gain a sense of 'reality' and shut things out, while children remain open. My mother has often told me that not long after her father died, she woke in the middle of the night on a few occasions to find me awake and standing in my cot talking. On one occasion, I pointed to a musical ornament that was sitting on her window ledge. It was of a boy and girl dancing and it played the song 'The Way We Were'. As I pointed, apparently I said, 'Man and lady dance,' and the ornament started to play as if it had been wound up!

I hope her mother was enlightened!

On another occasion when Sarah's mother found her talking at night and asked who she was chatting to she explained, 'It was the man at the bottom of the bed.' Sarah takes up the story:

> When she told me there was no man, I insisted, 'The man's there, at the bottom of the bed.' My mother often wonders if this was her father who'd popped over from the afterlife to visit his little grandchild.
>
> Years on, my sister moved into a new home near to our house. She had been very close to my grandfather and the last to see him alive. She now has children of her own and for a long time felt a presence in her home which she was sure was Grandfather. He had died in a house fire and she always smelled smoke when she felt the presence.

The children in the family, as is fairly typical, were also aware of his presence:

> Some time after they'd moved in, her daughter, then three, came downstairs and asked, 'What's the man doing upstairs?' She then led my sister upstairs to where the man was. There was no one there – at least my sister could see no one. She also experienced items going missing from her home and turning up some days later in another place or even in their original place.

Sarah confided that her mother and sister had both visited psychics who had told them that their grandfather had visited both of their homes:

> One even said that he was telling him there had been a problem with one of the taps in the kitchen. Sure enough, we had had a problem with our hot water tap in recent weeks!

Tom the Guardian Angel

Amanda was just a young girl when her father passed away:

> I was four or five years old when he took his own life. To this day I do not know the full story; my mother never has spoken about my father. All I know is she remarried a few weeks after his cremation and my new stepfather was an evil man.

The sadness of her father's passing remained with Amanda for many years and she didn't have an easy childhood:

> All my life I wondered what my father would have thought of us all. Would he have been proud of how we had all turned out? (I have four older brothers.) So many questions, and all unanswered.

Much later on, soon after she had got divorced, Amanda was feeling quite low one night:

> While I was trying to sleep I asked my father why he took his own life, why I had to grow up never knowing him and whether he was happy with us all.
>
> I'm not sure if it really was a voice in my head or whether I told myself what I really wanted to hear, but I felt he said he was sorry for what he had done and he was proud of all of us. It was as if I heard my father's voice in my head and it did bring me some comfort.
>
> Then, when my son was a few weeks old and my daughter Bekki was two years old, she started saying a man was sitting on her bed at night keeping her awake. I didn't take a lot of notice at the time. I was still feeding my son and I was becoming exhausted and so was my daughter.

Amanda's sleep depravation was causing her a lot of problems. Any mum will understand what this extreme tiredness feels like. One day it resulted in a serious incident, as Amanda explains:

> One morning my son woke up at 5 a.m. This was something he'd begun to do on a regular basis. I went to get him out of bed and through sheer tiredness I moaned that I might as well stay up every night as I never got any sleep. I got to the top of the stairs and next thing I remember is being at the bottom. Luckily I still had my son in my arms,

but I had cracked my coccyx. I don't even remember falling, just one thud and I was on the last-but-one step. I know for sure that someone saved us.

Amanda remembers another night that something strange happened:

I was putting Bekki to bed and the room was chilly, as always. Bekki told me the man was sitting on the bed again. I asked her to point to him but I couldn't see anything. I called him T.O.M. (The Old Man) and I told him he could protect the children but not to keep waking them up, as they needed their sleep.

Strangely enough, they never had a problem after that, but I did mention it to a neighbour and she told me the grandfather of the previous occupants used to look after the children while his daughter went to work. Rather bizarrely, his name was Tom and he had died in the house. Yet I felt sure that I had just made up the name!

Maybe it was a coincidence, yet there was more to come. When Amanda's children were about six or seven years old their great grandmother died:

About a week after the funeral my daughter got up one morning and said she had seen Great Nanny B. in a dream and she had been holding Michael. I asked who Michael was and she said, 'My brother.' My first child was stillborn at 26 weeks and my daughter had never been told she had an older brother, least of all that we had named him Michael.

Children seem so very aware of things that we ourselves do not. It might be worth paying a little more attention when the little ones in your life start chatting to their 'invisible friends'!

CHAPTER 6

Angels and Animals

Lots of people talk to animals ... not very many listen, though ... That's the problem.

Benjamin Hoff, *The Tao of Pooh*

The fun thing about animals is that sometimes they can be our angels too! Our furry friends like to help us both from this side of life and when they pass over to the light. Stories in my files include pets who have rescued their owners, animals who have appeared to their owners after they have died and those who have shown they are still around to watch over their owners as animal angels.

My own special little dog appeared to me in a dream visitation after she passed over. In the dream she was with all the other family dogs we had lost over the years and I always joke that if dogs could smile then smile is what she was doing! I know it sounds silly, but it wasn't as if she appeared like a cartoon dog – the smile was something that was shining from within her. Lady was a Lancashire heeler, a small black-and-tan-coloured dog, and I'd chosen her as the closest dog to a cat! I'll be honest, we were looking for a guard dog at the time and I'm really a cat fan, but Lady stole my heart. She was the sweetest little thing.

Sadly, as the end of her life was getting close I had to do what so many pet owners have to do – make a decision about whether to take her to the vet's so that he could end her life with dignity. I felt so guilty on her last day and laid all her favourite foods out on the floor so that she could eat whatever she wanted to. She kept looking up at me in disbelief and you could almost hear her saying, 'Mum, can I really eat whatever I want?'

One of my daughters accompanied me on her last ever walk and the biggest of tears streamed down my face. After the vet gave Lady a lethal injection I cried even more and the vet discretely withdrew as I said my last goodbyes. I actually curled her up on the table to make her *more comfortable,* even though she'd died already. It's funny the things that you do, isn't it?

In the days that followed, our ginger tomcat Tigger grieved too. He walked around the house as if he were looking for someone. I felt so responsible – I know everyone does. Grief and guilt are a difficult combination. So you can imagine how comforted I felt when Lady appeared to me in the dream to show me she was safe and well. Although I have written about this before, I think it's important that I share the story again here – and keep you up to date!

Shortly after Lady died, I happened to be interviewing the psychic artist Debbie Dean. Debbie specializes in drawing pictures of the spirits who visit her, giving tangible proof of what she sees with her inner eye to those who come to her for psychic readings. Whilst we were chatting on the telephone about her work she told me that she could see a little black dog running around her feet and that she thought that she might belong to me. I didn't want to get too excited, so asked her if she would be able to sketch the dog and e-mail me the image over. I didn't mention that my own little dog had recently died, and didn't want to give her any indication that I recognized the dog. I trusted Debbie totally, but this had to come from her. Could it be another sign from my little dog that she had made it safely to the other side?

About an hour later Debbie's drawing arrived in my inbox and I immediately printed it off. Without saying a word, I showed the picture to my elder daughter. The likeness to Lady was so accurate that my daughter immediately started crying. I know that my pet came back to let me know that she was safe and well on the other side.

Many months later I started having dreams of acquiring a new kitten. I knew that I would never buy another dog again. The kitten in my dreams was a little ginger tom and I knew that I would have to wait six weeks for him, as six weeks was the timing shown in the dream. I already had a ginger tomcat at home, so it was strange that I would see another cat just like it in my dreams.

I often wondered if my own angels had been leading the way when six weeks to the day my friend took me out for the day to a local craft shop at a working farm. We were shocked when we discovered that the farm had two ginger kittens for sale – one male and one female. I was ready to take the male home right away, but the carer insisted on keeping them for another week.

I was restless and when I was unable to contact the carer during the following week I turned up unexpectedly at the craft shop. The farm shop was actually closed, but I could see the distressed carer walking around with a bowl of food. She was calling out the names of the kittens and the mother cat was mewing in distress. It turned out that both kittens had disappeared. They'd been missing for several days, which is why the carer hadn't returned my calls. I was even more upset when she told me that a fox had been spotted round the farm rubbish bins, probably searching for food for its own young.

I hoped that someone who loved kittens had stolen them away. I didn't dare think of the alternative. After weeks of dreaming of a ginger kitten entering our home, I now felt like a mother bird with an empty nest. I quickly started to slide into depression and my own mother pointed out that I was grieving for a kitten I had never even owned! But that kitten had been promised to me in a dream and something had gone terribly wrong. I now understood my instinct to take him home right away. I was very, very upset.

Several weeks went by and I knew that I had to find another kitten to save my sanity, so I began to telephone round the local cat rescue centres to see if they had kittens ready for rehoming. I decided on a cat that was completely different from the one I *should* have had. Forget mystical dreams – this choice was to be a logical one only. My husband, who wasn't keen on having another cat at all, said grudgingly, 'Well, if I *had* to have a cat I would want a black one,' and I thought that if I was *going* to have a cat I would like a female one this time.

Several of the cat fosterers had kittens, but after much work it was discovered that there was only one black female kitten in the area. I asked over the phone for her to be saved for me and went to visit the very next day. As I walked into the house it was positively filled with giggling children and scampering kittens. All the kittens had white markings and splashes of other colour on their very fluffy fur. All were beautiful, just like kittens should look, and all 'photo ready' – perfect. But they were all male.

Then they brought out the female for me to inspect. She was much smaller than the other kittens and she had strange brown fur. She really was the weakling of the litter and to be honest she wasn't terribly attractive, bless her.

They placed this scruffy brown kitten on the sofa next to me and she immediately crawled along towards my lap, where she plonked herself down regally and promptly started to purr. This little kitten had the loudest purr I had ever heard and I fell in love with her immediately. This was my new cat. And although I'd chosen her in advance, just to be on the safe side, she'd now chosen me too.

Ear mites and other problems meant that there were two separate delays in picking her up and, as you can imagine, after losing one kitten I was in a bit of a panic about losing another. I knew that another woman had called asking for a black female kitten and the carers were also moving house. In the end I all but marched up to snatch her away. But then, just when I thought I couldn't stand to wait any longer, I was told I could pick her up and take her home with me. Of course with all the worry of losing the kitten, a most useful bonding experience had just taken place. It didn't matter what was wrong with her, she was mine and I wanted her, and I was taking her home right now.

'Magik' soon settled into her new surroundings. She was funny and intelligent, and it was strange how much she reminded us of our little dog Lady. Lady had been terrible about removing tissues from the wastepaper basket and shredding them up all over the floor. Magik began doing the same thing. Magik would also lie along the back of the sofa just like Lady and there were other things that made us laugh and reminded us of our old dog. At one time she had four front teeth where her milk teeth and her adult teeth were sharing the same space in her mouth at the same time.

One night I had another dream visitation. Lady came to me again. This time she morphed into a kitten and back again. What was she trying to tell me? Then she showed me her front teeth and two of them fell out of her mouth. I got it! She was trying to show me that she had reincarnated as my cat – how bizarre! OK, I know this sounds crazy, but everything suddenly made so much sense. Lady had clearly had the opportunity to come back to us again. The scruffy brown and black fur, the shredding of tissues – they were all signs. Lady had become Magik! Our dog had come back as our cat and yes, when I checked the next morning, the four front teeth had become two, just as I had been shown in the dream. Our kitten had lost her extra teeth and I feel that I was shown it at that exact time because it would be proof that my dream experience was real.

Magik is now 12 months old and her scruffy fur has given way to the most beautiful black shiny coat. She's still small, but very agile. She no longer shreds paper from the wastepaper bin, thank goodness! She's very special.

At night when I write my books in the conservatory, which I call my 'office at home', I have company. I have two basket chairs in my room and even if I work late into the night or start early in the morning, the cats stay with me. Most of the time Magik sits curled in one chair and my big ginger tomcat Tigger snoozes in the other. Occasionally they curl up together and from time to time they sit on the desk in front of me to check that I am OK or to get a little tickle behind the ears. It's as if they feel I need some sort of reassurance: 'Go on, Mum, keep going with the book …'

Like all pet owners, I think my animals are my angels, but I know for sure that I had a little divine intervention to get them into my life. I even have a photograph of Lady wearing a pair of angel wings after the children dressed her up one day. She's certainly my angel on the other side of life. I also have the beautiful sketch drawn by the psychic artist Debbie Dean and you can view it, along with a photograph of my little dog, at her website (www.debbiedean.org.uk). And is a part of her spirit inside my beautiful little kitten Magik? It certainly seems possible!

Isn't it amazing how animals bring us such friendship – even birds? If you're not an animal fan it's hard to understand how each pet has such a different personality and the effect they can have on us. You would be amazed at how many people write and tell me, 'If it wasn't for my dog/cat/horse/any pet you can think of, I wouldn't be here today' or 'I would never have got through this time.' Never underestimate the power of a pet to put things right …

I always love reading stories of these magical animal 'angels'. Here are a few of them.

One Last Time

Esther is from Holland. She wrote:

> My mother's blond Bouvier dog Iris was 15 years old when she suddenly passed away. Mum rang me when she thought her time was close, so I got in the car and drove to her house, an hour and a half's journey, to be with her. Sadly, when I arrived Iris had already passed away.
>
> Iris was such a big part of the family that I felt really bad that I hadn't been with her to say goodbye. But there was nothing more that I could have done.
>
> Two days later, as my husband and I were going to bed I gave him a goodnight kiss and then realized that someone was in the room with us. I looked up and there was Iris at the foot of the bed. Her coat was so shiny and white and she looked so beautiful, surrounded by a white light. I was so happy that I had the opportunity to see her one last time and I really thank her for that.

Ghost Dog in a Tornado

My friend the past-life expert and author Jenny Smedley originally alerted me to this special story and I contacted dog-owner Jill so she could share her experience with me. If you ever think your pets leave you for good after they pass over, then think again. When Jill found herself in severe danger and was frightened and alone, her special dog Sampson came back for a visit from his heavenly home so that she could be comforted at the time that she needed it most.

Before I tell you about her experience, let me tell you about Sampson. Jill described her unusual little dog for me:

> He was a tiny mutt, a nondescript mixed breed of dog who weighed at most 12lbs. His name was Sampson, but the family named him 'the Mighty Sampson' because he always thought he was such a big tough boy.

Sampson had the appearance of a black Labrador retriever – a small one, of course! Jill said she called him her 'funny little Sammy'. He was a very protective dog and especially protective of her. He wouldn't let strangers near her, was particularly wary of men and would snap and growl until Jill told him that people were safe. Sammy was a tiny dog, but he was always a furry guardian angel to Jill.

Jill and Sampson were a part of each other's lives from when she was 21 until she was 39. She explains, 'He was always with me, just like a child, and when he died in 1999 I was devastated. He had been my baby and I never ever wanted to have another pet.'

Jill missed Sampson terribly, but he hadn't gone far away after all. His protective instincts meant that he was around whenever she wanted his support.

Late in the spring of 2000 there were terrible storms in the southern United States. In the past when thunderstorms or any other violent weather threatened, Sampson had always curled up next to Jill to keep her safe. Now Jill was missing his protection. His touch and presence were always such a comfort to her. This particular night, at about three in the morning, thunder was crashing and wind was slashing against the windows and doors. Jill said:

> I woke up, certain I was hearing a tornado. You're in the UK, right? I guess you don't have those over there. They are terrifying storms which are caused by the clash of warm air meeting with cold air, usually in the spring, forming swirling funnel clouds which can cause utter devastation. When people describe them as the sound of a freight train roaring through, they aren't exaggerating.

Jill is right, this type of weather is not normal in the UK, so it was hard for me to understand the terror of the storm she must have experienced that night. But she didn't have to face it on her own after all. She explained:

> Right after I woke up I felt Sammy's warm fur under my hand. I immediately thought, 'Sammy, this is scary. Good

dog for being with Mama!' and I curled up with his fur under my hand and prayed we would not be hit by this tornado.

Sampson felt so real that Jill forgot for a moment that he was no longer on this Earth. She remembers:

Then I woke up completely and realized Sammy could not be there in his physical form, but I still felt his fur under my fingers just as real as day. My heart started pounding ... Sampson? Before I had much time to think, I felt a movement away from me, down the bed. It was as though all the air was being sucked out of the room and I felt this – how can I describe it? It was a rushing away feeling. My heart was pounding, but then I realized the storm had just as suddenly passed over.

Jill was left more than a little bemused about what had happened. 'I kept thinking I must have been crazy,' she said. She knew the experience had been real, though, and that her darling little dog had been with her during the storm, even if it had been as a ghost dog:

When I woke up, my heart was lighter and no longer aching for my little Sammy. Because I knew he'd been there with me and always will be.

The next day Jill realized she'd had a close call:

I found out in the daylight hours the apex of the storm hit a mere few miles from me. The officials never called it a tornado, though, they called it 'straight line winds', which is a fancy way of saying it blew some roofs off nearby buildings and it actually destroyed one business completely.

Now Jill knows in her heart and in her head that if she needs him, 'the Mighty Sampson' will be her guardian. And she says, 'I am firmly convinced he came back to ease my worries about the storm.'

The Healing Angel

Penny's dog Angel (yes, that really was her name) was born dead. This poor little pup had died before she had even left the womb, but Penny jumped to the rescue and with more than a little effort managed to revive the struggling little puppy.

If you can imagine the bond that might exist between an owner and the pup she miraculously brought back to life, you will have some understanding of how close Penny is to her dog. Angel literally owed her life to Penny and she has shown her gratitude over and over again. Penny told me:

We've had Angel for ten years now and her love is beyond belief. She knows when you are sad and need cheering up.

> Life with Angel was great at first but then we had some personal problems at home. About two years ago my husband became deeply depressed. Things became so bad that he seriously considered taking his own life. I don't know how she knew, but Angel seemed to sense this. Our beautiful and loving dog just would not leave my husband alone.

Angel had a task to do. She was picking up a distress signal from one of her beloved owners. Penny explained:

> I was out at work and Angel clearly felt she had to keep my husband alive until I got home and was able to take over. She kept kissing him to the point of almost being a pest and there was no way that she would allow him anywhere near the gas oven or the pills. Angel literally saved his life by just giving him the love he needed to help see him through. Thankfully he is well again now, but without Angel I might not have a husband.

Angel does seem particularly sensitive to the humans around her and this wasn't her only act of healing, as Penny confided:

> About five years ago I was not feeling well at all. I was suffering from what I thought was severe indigestion. I really felt very poorly, but I was 'putting a brave face on it'. Angel, being Angel, knew there was something the matter.

She kept nuzzling me and pawing my stomach. Throughout this whole time she would not leave my side and refused to even go out for walks.

The pain just went on for days and then one particular night it was so very bad that it was keeping me awake. I didn't want to wake my husband up because he had an early start at work the following morning and I was trying to suffer in silence. But Angel knew that I was seriously ill and she eventually woke Bill. I was rushed to hospital and had an emergency operation to remove my gallbladder! It seems that my 'indigestion' was a little worse than I had first thought!

'My Angel Animals Saved Me from Depression'

Dorothy lives in the USA and her animals were so special that I felt compelled to share her story with you here. At a time when her life was in deep turmoil, her pets helped her to keep it together.

Dorothy told me:

I don't really have a miracle story, but to me it seemed like a miracle at the time. It all started when my husband of 22 years decided he didn't want to be married anymore. The phrase he used was, 'I love you but I don't want to live with you anymore.' A bit of a shock, I must say.

When you are a family with animals, it's a little like having children, and pets can complicate a relationship split too. Dorothy continued:

> About a year before we had adopted the love of our life, an umbrella cockatoo we named Bongo. She was our child and gave us a lot of joy. But when things started to go badly for us, Bongo was very upset.

Animals are very sensitive, as we have already discovered. It's amazing how much they become aware of tension in a home:

> Just as a two-year-old human child would react to seeing its parents constantly angry at each other, Bongo just couldn't understand why her 'parents' couldn't get along. She was intensely bonded to my husband and when we separated, we agreed that he should take her.

But finding the ideal solution to custody is not easy, as any 'parent' will tell you. Dorothy explained:

> He went on frequent trips and when he was not in town Bongo stayed with me. At the time I worked in an office which was moved from downtown Washington, DC, to New Carrollton, MD. The move meant that I now had to commute nearly four hours per day to get to work. Also, there are only two ways to get across the Potomac river

from Maryland – two bridges. One night a distraught man decided he would jump from the top of one of them. Traffic was stopped and nobody was going anywhere as the man argued for hours with police.

Sad as this situation was, Dorothy was concerned about Bongo:

After hours in the traffic jam, I was looking forward to seeing Bongo, who was staying with me for a few days. When I opened the door, I immediately saw her cage door was open (Bongo was always the best at getting out of her cage – especially those billed as 'bird proof'). I was exhausted after spending over three hours on the road home, added to the ten hours on the job and the two-hour commute in. It was nearly 9 o'clock at night and I had to track Bongo down.

Bongo had been busy during the day and made an enormous mess:

I followed a trail of thrown cat toys, magazines and chewed-on baseboards and drywall. I walked up the stairs past the snacked-on banisters and into my bedroom, where the clean laundry had been tossed all over the room. Next I walked into the master bathroom, where I found the bird and the mess. Everything that could have been thrown on the floor was. Bongo was atop the shower rod covered in makeup obviously very happy with herself.

An exhausted Dorothy was now at breaking-point:

> My husband of over two decades had left me because he wanted to date other people, my job had moved to a location where I needed to spend hours just to get to the job then worked a ten-hour day and then it was taking me hours to get home. Then to come home to a total disaster created by a bored cockatoo? I was at the end of my tether.

Have you ever had days like that? I know I have. Dorothy explained:

> I couldn't take it anymore. I just sat down in the middle of the mess and cried. It was then that Bongo hopped down from the shower rod and over to me. She climbed up into my lap and gave me a kiss, saying, 'I love you!' Bongo was clearly feeling guilty!
>
> For me that was my animal miracle. It was pretty obvious by now that my husband and I would not get back together (the girlfriend sort of hinted at that) and Bongo was his bird, so I had to give her back, but when I did, the house was so horribly quiet I just had to go and get a bird of my own.

Dorothy was careful to make sure she found a good bird:

> I went to a very reputable breeder. In their office they encourage potential customers to play with the birds and

interact with them and I was drawn to the cage of a very young Moluccan cockatoo (the largest of the white cockatoos), who still had much of her baby down. I opened the cage door and she ran right up my arm and nuzzled under my chin and the only thing she knew how to say was 'I love you' – perfect!

Ruffles came home with me that week and has been a great comfort ever since. She was very sweet as I injected baby gruel into her crop every morning and night. She was able to eat on her own but preferred her baby gruel and was young enough for me to indulge her as one would a toddler who doesn't want to give up the bottle completely.

At last Dorothy had her own bird, but things are never that easy, are they?

Near this time I sensed that my husband might not want to keep Bongo after all. He was travelling a lot, so I told him that I really wanted her back since she was my bird too.

Bongo wasn't pleased!

This was the final straw for her. She adored Peter and now not only had she lost her family, but her 'person' didn't want her any more. She was very upset about this. To this day, Peter is the only man she allows near her except for a friend who looks a little like him. But by now my job was taking me away for longer and longer during the day and Bongo finally decided that Ruffles was pretty good company after all. Now they're inseparable.

So it seems that things worked out in the end. Dorothy says:

Now when I come home from work, I open the door and I hear, 'Hi, Mommy! I love you!' What could be better than that? With the divorce there were many days that Ruffles and Bongo gave me a reason to get up in the morning. When I was feeling very down, they would sleep with me and every few hours would wake me with a kiss that meant 'Take me to the potty.' Honestly, with everything that has happened since, I believe that these two cockatoos are the only things that have kept me from even considering giving up.

The cockatoos have become Dorothy's animal angels:

They make me laugh, they comfort me when I cry and they stay with me when I'm sick. Bongo has learned to give a high four (only four toes), to say 'Buk, buk, buk' like a chicken, play bat and 'Flap-flap wings', and has picked the lock on every cage I've bought her. I got one of her cages free because the vendor didn't believe she could get out of it. I told her that Bongo would absolutely get out and the lady told me that if she did they'd send free locks for life to replace the ones Bongo picked. We're on our third set now.

Over the years the angel crew began to grow. Dorothy explains:

> I've had my birds for about 12 years now and my little family also contains three cats. Yeti is an albino who is deaf and was a kitten at the same time as Ruffles was a baby, so the two of them will play together. Maynard G. Krebbs is a black-and-white cat with a small black goatee. He's nearly 18 now. Smidgen, the baby, is a tiny two-year-old calico with a tail about an inch long and kinked like a pig's. She is the sweetest little thing and always purring. She likes it when the birds preen her, but can't understand why cockatoos don't like being licked by cats!

You know, I really believe that when God can't provide the human company we need, he gives us pets. Dorothy agrees:

> I love them all dearly. Ruffles is such fun and always runs to me with a scarf we call the 'peekaboo' cloth. Peekaboo is her favourite game. She'll bring the cloth and say, 'Mommy, wanna play peekaboo?' When we play I cover each pet in turn and say 'Where's Yeti, or whoever?' and she will run and pull the cloth off and say, 'Peekaboo, Whoever!'
>
> So there you have it, my family. I wouldn't trade them for a *real* one for anything. And a word of warning: any guy who is interested in me takes us all as a package. Maybe it sounds cold, but my animals kept me from sinking into

depression when my husband left, and you don't reward that kind of loyalty by taking them to the animal shelter when it's not convenient to keep them anymore. In fact, my birds are willed to a neighbour they adore. She sits for them when I'm on work trips. She loves them very much and makes them little treats and plays with them every time she's here, so she spoils them rotten.

Many people wonder how cats co-exist with cockatoos. It only took one bite on the end of each of their too inquisitive noses to teach them respect. And it didn't take long to learn that lesson either!

Dorothy's family of animal angels sounds adorable, but I bet your pets are just as cute and loving!

The Bee

My friend Jill Wellington, the American author and TV presenter, told me this fun little story recently:

In the past few weeks I noticed a single bee would come and buzz around my face. I hate bees! Nobody else seemed to attract this bee and to be honest it was beginning to scare me. I started to get all upset trying to swat it away all the time.

Jill believes in angels, so thought she would ask for some help. She told me:

Yesterday, I decided to ask my guardian angel to take the bee away from me. As it was hovering around my face, I decided to stay perfectly still and ask for help. Imagine how stunned I was as I watched the bee simply turn around and fly off! It was astounding!

Jill said that the bee never bothered her again. Perhaps you might like to try this method with your own insect pests! You never know …

Butterflies

Clare e-mailed over a story after we met at a special training group I ran for counsellors at a local hospice. She wrote:

I didn't feel it was right to share an experience with you on the night because I was a visitor, although so many things that you said 'struck a chord' with me. Strange things have happened to me since I was a teenager and I have taken a great interest in spiritual matters over the years. I'd like to tell you of an experience I had with butterflies.

Last August my partner's father, Tom, passed away. He was taken into hospital on the Friday and was due to have tests done the following Monday. I should have visited him on the Sunday with my partner and his daughter, but I chose not to go at the last minute.

He took a turn for the worse on the Sunday evening and wasn't well enough to have the tests. I then came down with a cold and as Tom was in the hospital ICU, it was sensible for me not to visit and sadly I never got the chance to say goodbye.

I'd only known Tom for about 18 months and hadn't really got to know him properly. I felt a little sad about this and I wrote a little letter to go into his coffin just to say goodbye and to let him know that I was sorry we hadn't known each other longer.

About a month after Tom's passing I was visiting my partner's mother at the family home. We were talking about Tom when the smoke alarm went off downstairs. We all laughed and jokingly said that it was Tom. While I was standing on a chair, trying to turn the alarm off, the smoke alarm at the top of the stairs started ringing too. Now we *knew* it was Tom!

The following week I walked into the lounge and there was a white feather on the carpet, which I took to be another little sign, but during this whole time it was still playing on my mind that I hadn't said goodbye.

At the end of September I took part in a healing course. One Saturday in October the house was quiet, so I gave myself a healing treatment lasting about an hour. I relaxed quite deeply into it and felt as though I was floating outside my body until reality brought me back again.

It was a glorious day and following my treatment I went outside to put the washing on the line. As I moved the line prop, a red admiral butterfly flew off. It startled me for a second, but I thought nothing more of it and carried on hanging out the washing. Within seconds the butterfly returned to sit on the prop and stayed there for the duration of my work.

This butterfly seemed particularly interested in the washing and I managed to get within six inches of it before it flew off and then returned to the prop. By this time I was starting to think that it was a sign from a loved one, but then as I put the prop back up it flew away.

I walked up the path in deep thought and the butterfly came back, flying beside me all the way, and settled on the wall of the conservatory. I sat outside enjoying the sunshine for half an hour talking to the butterfly and found that it would open its wings as if in reply to my questions. It did seem particularly friendly!

The butterfly remained on the wall all afternoon and I really felt that this was Tom coming to say goodbye and let me know he was OK. In fact I feel closer to him now, because I can share my thoughts with him.

I do still feel that Tom is around me even now. Last night I was in the dining room on the computer when at 11.15 p.m. my daughter Lucy, aged two and half, got up crying and asking to go to the toilet. I went up to see to her and then put her back in bed, but when I came back downstairs again all the lights had been switched on! I know when I went up the only lights on were the wall lights in the dining room and the landing light, because the hall was quite dark. Spirits at play, maybe?

The Robin

I receive a lot of stories about birds. Many people believe birds to be signs of spirit who often appear around the time of a death and again immediately afterwards. Robins are very friendly anyway, but do seem to feature a lot in the experiences that people share with me.

Jan had a robin experience of her own. She told me, 'A friend who was working at the same school as me sadly passed with cancer.'

Jan wasn't looking for a sign, but felt that what happened next was certainly significant:

> The day before her funeral I was walking through the school when a robin flew straight through the open door in front of me and perched on a bookcase to my left. He stared me out, then flew very gently into my friend's classroom and perched on her desktop. He sat there staring at me before gracefully flying up and then down before going out through the open window.

Even for a robin the bird was acting in a very unusual way. Could this be a sign of some sort? Jan continues:

> It is a very old school and the windows are the old type that make it virtually impossible to fly through without doing somersaults. This robin knew exactly where he was going. I was completely spellbound by his movements and knew

> instantly that he had been sent as a messenger from my friend to let me know she was OK.

The message managed to simply convey that her teacher friend was safe and well in her new home in the afterlife. Like many signs of this sort, the unusual behaviour of an animal or bird is a gentle and non-frightening way of reaching out to us from the other side of life.

'I felt no grief after that,' Jan said, 'and just wanted to tell her husband not to worry and that she was fine. I knew she was. Sadly he doesn't believe in anything like this and would think I was crazy, so I kept the experience to myself.'

Jan has had other experiences too. She told me:

> I believe all animals have a sixth sense. I had my Alsatian Sheba for 14 years and we were so in tune it was unbelievable. She seemed to know my every thought and I hers. If I thought about her, whether about feeding her or taking her out, or indeed anything, she would instantly make a noise in response.

I've researched this phenomenon in the past and found it often happens with young children who have no language available to them. Pets, like children, find another way to communicate. I believe that animals can literally 'see' our thoughts on occasion.

Sheba visited Jan after she died too:

When she passed, especially in the months after, I would feel her get on the bed and she would nuzzle my hands. I knew she was still with me.

Although I believe without a doubt that we go on to another dimension, I must say in all honesty that I haven't seen an angel yet, although I would love to. I would also love to be in touch with my guardian angel, but if I ever need help with my son then I talk to my angels and, boy, do I get results!

I agree! Like the bee story before, it's worth asking your guardian angels to help in any given situation. You might be surprised at the results too!

... and Another Robin Story

As I said, I get a lot of bird stories, so I thought I would include another robin experience here. It makes you feel there has to be something going on, right? Robins are definitely designated messengers!

Sue was reading an angel robin story in my last book and was prompted to write to me:

My dear dad passed away almost four years ago, actually on the day of the Queen Mother's funeral. He was 87 years old and for many years we were not particularly close due to the fact that I was only 15 when my mother died (I'm nearly 57 now) and Dad remarried fairly swiftly after, which to my tender years seemed far too soon. I must add here that my step-mom was a really nice lady and I came to love her as such in the later years.

Sue and her dad had tried to work on their relationship before he passed, though. She explained:

To cut a long story short, Dad became very ill with cancer a couple of years before his death and we once again became close. I did my level best to do whatever I could in the way of caring for him. I took him to hospital appointments, called in every other morning to shave him (which his regular carer used to save for me to do, knowing that's what I wanted), and so it went on until Dad was too ill and had to be hospitalized.

From then on I went religiously every evening to feed him and give him his tablets. At the end, because my step-mom was too frail to look after him, he went into a nursing home, but sadly only for one day. I was the one who found him when he died, in his room at the nursing home.

Sue was naturally devastated:

Of course this was so upsetting, I'd been to see him in the morning and shaved him, even though he was asleep ready for his next visitors (my step-mom and step-sister). I had planned to go back after work, which of course I did, but sadly I was too late. I was comforted, though, by the fact that I had been the one to find him.

It was a few weeks later that Sue felt her father had brought her a sign:

> I was in the living room and our dog started to make a fuss in the dining room, so I rushed in to see what was going on. I couldn't believe my eyes. There on the windowsill, sitting right by my dad's photo, was a little robin. I was bewildered. I couldn't even begin to think how this little robin had managed to find his way through the kitchen door and into the dining room.
>
> I spoke very gently to him and asked if he was there for a reason. And this I found truly amazing – he actually let me pick him up and he sat on the palm of my hand and allowed me to carry him outside! All the time I was stroking him and speaking to him. I then said, 'OK, little bird, you're free to fly away now,' and off he went.
>
> I'm sure this was my dad letting me know he was OK. I certainly like to think so. Naturally since this time robins have been my special bird.

Animal Angels on Both Sides of Life

Tracey wrote to me from England. Like Dorothy in the earlier story, animals of all sorts, from both sides of life, seem to have featured in her life. She also has some human angels and they watch over the animals too. She told me:

When my granddad died about 14 years ago, my mother and I were devastated. We were both so close to him and I never got to say goodbye to him, as he was taken into hospital suddenly. At the time I was living and working about 100 miles away and I just couldn't get home quickly enough.

Then, about two weeks after his death, my granddad appeared to me one night. It was so real. I was scared when I saw him, but he looked so well and appeared to me in the way I remember him from when I was a small child. He said to me, 'Don't be scared. I am well and not in pain anymore.' Then right afterwards he was gone.

The next day when I woke I felt so happy. It was as if a weight had lifted from me. I knew I had to tell my mum, as she was in such pain from losing him, so I phoned her up straight away. She was in tears and so happy when I told her.

Granddad's appearance certainly did the trick, but Tracey had more to share:

I have seen spirits before, but mainly animals. When I was a young child – I can't remember what age, maybe five or six – I saw the spirit of a dog. I actually woke up to see it at my bedside and as we didn't have any pets in our home at that time I knew it wasn't a real dog. I was scared at first, but then it came up to me and licked my hand before it disappeared. I always wondered why it happened, though.

Other pets visited Tracey in the night too:

> On another occasion I woke up and saw a black cat on the end of my bed. At first I thought it was real. I felt scared and told it to get off my bed, but it wouldn't go. I shut my eyes, but it was still there when I opened them again, so I called out to my mum and dad. My dad came into my bedroom and the cat disappeared. I told him about it, but he didn't believe me. As soon as he had gone, the cat came back onto my bed! I called out again and my dad came into the room again and it disappeared again. My dad still didn't believe me. I never saw the cat again. But I still can remember it so vividly even now I am 35.
>
> I now have two real cats, both Burmese. I love them to bits, but they are very naughty and hyperactive. Fidget, my red, has gone missing a couple of times, but one time I was really worried when he hadn't come home at midday. He always comes home for a bite to eat and Burmese love human company, so I knew immediately something was wrong.
>
> I started to call out for him and I looked everywhere and by the evening I was really worried. My partner and I started walking around the fields, as we live in a rural area. We walked for miles and miles. It was about 10 p.m. and we decided to give up for the night. Of course I couldn't sleep. I stayed awake all night listening for my Fidget to cry at the door to be let in.
>
> When the sun rose in the morning I got up. It was about 6 a.m. and I decided to walk around the fields again, this

time shouting til my voice was sore. I started crying and in desperate plea I decided to ask 'someone' to help me – God or maybe a spirit, perhaps even Granddad? I still couldn't find Fidget and went home with tears in my eyes. My partner had tears in his eyes too when he saw how upset I was, so we decided to go out looking for him again at 8 a.m.

This time we split up and I had this strange urge to go back to the field where I had been looking in the morning. I started to feel as if I was being led and felt drawn right to the edge of the field. The wind had picked up and I had to really shout out Fidget's name. As I stopped for breath I heard a faint noise. Could that be a cat's meow? I called out again and this time I heard a faint meow. My heart started beating faster and faster as I shouted again and again. I walked towards the sound of the meow, but I couldn't see anything. Then I looked up and stuck up the tree was Fidget!

I couldn't believe it. I'd been led right to the very spot and I know I'd have never have found him otherwise. I was literally standing right underneath the tree before I could hear anything at all!

Tracey was now one very relieved owner. The chances of her finding the cat by 'accident' were fairly slim indeed. Of course she still had to get Fidget out of the tree! She told me:

He looked very scared and must have been in the tree all night. I was so happy that I had found him and luckily I had taken my mobile phone with me and was able to call my partner, who fetched a ladder to rescue him. As soon as we got him down, he purred like crazy!

I know now that I definitely had help in finding him and the very next day I found a white feather. It's really nice to know we are being helped by our loved ones and angels on the other side, isn't it? Maybe Fidget has his own angel?

Crash!

Do our pets have their own guardian angels? I firmly believe that they do. As with humankind, each animal has a guardian who watches over them. My own kitten Magik certainly has help from her angels. We call her a 'little monkey' because she is always getting into mischief.

Just this week my husband called me to tell me he had heard a massive crash from our bedroom. Magik had jumped into my bedroom window and pulled down the lace curtain, bending the curtain rod completely. A large gold-framed mirror had been pulled down along with the curtain, and several cut-crystal glasses which I use to keep cotton wool pads and cosmetic brushes in. Most of the contents of my make-up bag was scattered on the floor too.

Nothing was broken – not even the kitten! I laughed hysterically when I walked into the bedroom. My two cats were lying side by side next to each other on the bed. They seemed to have a fake innocent look on their faces as if to say, 'Who, us?' We all know that cats would normally have run away from the noise, but perhaps not when one of them was to blame!

Strangely enough, an angel figurine that I'd had in the bedroom for a year or so fell off the shelf about an hour later. Its poor wings had broken off and I sadly placed it in my wastepaper basket. It seemed to tell me that it had 'taken the fall' for my kitten. I never did find out how it fell off the shelf, but I think I can guess.

Magik also went skiing this week. '*Skiing*?' I hear you say. Yes, indeed. My husband John had placed a cardboard box on our landing at home for my elder daughter to sort some items into. I heard a sliding noise followed by a crash and Magik peeped over the top of the box, which was now at the bottom of the stairs. She'd used it for a ride down the stairs – although probably not on purpose! Once again she survived the experience unscathed.

Now I know why they say that cats have nine lives. Magik has used hers all up just this week!

A Little Call for Help

This story is extraordinary. Lucy wrote to tell me about a family friend's dog called Addie. Strange but true …

> My mum's friend has a beautiful dog, a black Scottie called Addie. She is a clever little thing as she is a 'care dog'. Her owner is now permanently wheelchair bound and Addie helps her pick things up and tells her when there is someone at the door and so on. Sadly, Addie is now getting old and starting to suffer with a few aches and pains, as dogs do.

Then disaster happened:

> One very early morning, at around 2 a.m. my mother was woken by the telephone ringing and a very distraught conversation followed. Addie had taken a turn for the worst in the night and appeared to be fitting and very ill. Mum immediately jumped in the car and went round to the house to help. Between the two of them she and her friend settled little Addie and contacted the vet, who said not to worry she would be OK, but to call again if she got worse.

Addie seemed to get no better and the two women were very worried:

> My mum's friend lives in a very quiet place and what happened next could not be put down to outside noise, especially not at that time of the night. Whilst her friend was making tea in the kitchen Mum was standing with her back to Addie, who was now in her basket. Out of nowhere she heard a desperate little voice say, 'Help me!'

Mum looked around and decided to put it down to being tired and stressed. But shortly afterwards she heard it again: 'Help ... help me.'

Had Addie somehow spoken? It seemed too weird, but maybe it wasn't? Lucy told me:

This little voice continued and Mum, not quite knowing what it was, searched madly around the little house, even opening the front door and looking out onto the street. When she ventured back inside the house she heard it again and, looking at the dog, she suddenly wondered, 'Could it be her?'

Taking no risks, she immediately advised her friend to contact the vet and they arranged for an emergency visit. It was lucky they did, because shortly afterwards poor Addie took another turn for the worse. The little voice literally saved her life and she then went on to make a full recovery.

Lucy told me:

I have to say that when Mum told me about the experience I wasn't surprised at all (although there were other members of the family who had a chuckle!) My mum has always believed in 'something else' being out there and we both think there was more to her experience that night than just being tired.

What a great story! Was the voice that of Addie or her angels? Who knows, but it certainly did the trick.

'Dream' Voice to the Rescue

This next story is about a small kitten like my own. Hayley wrote:

> This morning, whilst enjoying my Sunday morning *extra two hours* lie-in, I suddenly heard a child's voice shouting loudly in my ear, *'Hayley, get up!'* I woke up with a jump and realized that there was not a child in my room (and that my daughter was actually out at the time).
>
> Trying to track down the voice, I went to look out of our bedroom window and was shocked to see our littlest cat, five-month-old Zahara, trotting happily into the road. (She is not allowed out of the house until she's grown a few more brain cells!)

Hayley was frantic. She wasn't even dressed, but there was no one else in the house to help:

> My husband had gone over for his Sunday morning 'espresso-and-putting-the-world-to-rights' with his brothers and had obviously not noticed little Zahara slipping out of the door beside him.

Hayley was now very frightened. The road out the front was a very busy one and Zahara had no road sense at all. Hayley told me:

> I managed to get downstairs, down the path and out of the gate just in time to see a lorry come trundling towards her. I just managed to grab her as she had sat down on the white line in the middle of the road.

What on earth would have happened if the mystery voice hadn't woken Hayley up?

Ah, the trials and tribulations of a five-month-old kitten … Um, yes, that sounds familiar! Magik is not allowed out either, but still she escaped out of the door a couple of weeks ago when no one was looking. We always do a half-hour check and were worried when she didn't come when we called.

She'd managed to climb the fence in the garden, but then fallen between our fence panel and the neighbours', effectively making trapping herself as if in a cage. Luckily we spotted her. I was half-cross, but more relieved that she was OK and hadn't escaped into a neighbour's garden. We had to lift the panel out of place to reach her and when you see those little sad eyes looking up at you your heart just melts and you can't be cross for long. I suppose I will never be ready to let her out on her own. Kittens, huh?

Angel Eyes

Roz had a brief experience with sunshine and also a little encounter with a butterfly. Was this an angel sign too? She explained:

> This morning I woke to a very 'dreich' Scottish morning with the rain battering against the windowpanes. A small chink of sunshine was shining through a gap in the curtains and through the heading on the book on my bedside and the beautiful image of an angel was shining right into my eyes! I couldn't believe what I was seeing and kept closing my eyes, thinking it would disappear, but it kept on shining through!
>
> Eventually, the sunshine moved away and so did my 'angel'. For the rest of today we have had incessant rain, but I've had my 'moment', so am very happy! It was very comforting – and very strange! Maybe she will come back tomorrow morning?
>
> Also, whilst I was on the way to the doctor with my son today (still in the rain), a beautifully coloured butterfly flew right toward my driver's door. It just seemed an unusual thing for it to have done.

Butterflies are signs of spirit and often appear at the perfect time to bring reassurance and comfort.

The Rabbit and the Holy Water

Our pets are very special to us and nothing is more distressing than to see them become ill. Whatever they are, they are precious to us. Sherrie believes that Kismet is a very special friend indeed and e-mailed to tell me about him:

> One cold and frosty morning God sent me an 'angel': my husband was gently cupping a little bunny he had found in our front garden. The bunny was cold and wet and desperately in need of some tender loving care. I found an old eye-dropper to feed him with and soon he was lapping milk from my hand. My husband named him Kismet (meaning 'Fate') and I called him Bunny Blue and we kept him at home, where he just thrived.

As we know, a difficult start to life can create a very strong bond between pet and owner. Kismet was a very valuable little bundle indeed:

> Kismet grew into a big happy bunny and then disaster struck one evening when he was just four months of age. I was passing by his hutch when I saw that his little body was lifeless, and he was staring into space. His breathing was very heavy. He tried to move, but instead his body writhed in convulsions. I knew then that he had been affected by the dreaded Calici virus, the same evil that had

claimed the life of my mum's bunny, another foundling, just a week before.

I was simply terrified that Kismet would die and my heart ached. I didn't know what to do, so I just bundled him up and brought him inside the house. It was all he could do to take a little water in the side of his mouth from my finger and I was in utter despair. My beautiful Bunny Blue was dying. Who could help me now?

Sherrie believes in a higher power and knew it was worth asking for help:

Suddenly it came upon me, the only one who could help: our darling God. I hurried immediately into the kitchen to fetch my bottle of holy water. I'd kept it safe after my children's baptisms. With tears rolling down my face, I sprinkled the water over my Bunny Blue and looked to heaven and asked the Lord to do his will – to let him stay with me or, if he had to go, to please take him without pain.

Could God fight the virus with Bunny Blue?

At first I thought it might be just wishful thinking, but I thought I saw a hint of hope in my little bunny's eyes, a sudden spark that wasn't there before. I just prayed and prayed. The hours passed by and he was still ill, but somehow a little better. My little fellow fought on.

Sherrie decided to leave things in God's hands:

> I went to bed and prayed again and in the morning went to check on my sweet bunny. I was frightened of what I might see, but had faith that God would have taken care of him regardless.
>
> As I opened the door, my heart nearly burst with joy and tears began to flow down my face. There was my Bunny Blue sitting up in his bed. He tried his hardest to hop to me, even though he was still half-paralysed in his back legs. I knew this was the hand of God and I looked to the heavens and thanked him with all my might.

And now?

> Today Kismet is a healthy, happy, beautiful buck and I know each day when I look at him that what I am seeing is a miracle. It may mean nothing to some, but to me his recovery was and will always be one of those little miracles that some of us have been blessed to see.
>
> So I guess Kismet is a fitting name – fate to come to me and fate to be saved by the hand of God. Miracles can happen – we just have to believe.

Sherrie is right. I believe that it is important to ask for help from God and his angels. Angels are not permitted to intervene in our lives unless we give them permission

– except in extreme emergencies when it is *not* our time to go.

Our souls grow from the love we give and share. Imagine how much Sherrie loved Kismet to suggest that God take him if that was his will, to love him so much as to be prepared to let him go if it meant no pain. I know that Kismet is a very lucky bunny indeed.

Mr Bunny

Jamii is from Australia. Here is Mr Bunny's story:

Mr Bunny was a white semi-dwarf short-haired rabbit with dark brown ears and a bit of dark brown colour next to his nose. He was healthy, cheeky, and had loads of attitude. He died of natural causes on the last day of February 1999 around age eight.

From October the previous year right up to his passing of heart failure he seemed to age so rapidly. When he finally went I was absolutely devastated, even more so than I expected. For three days afterwards I couldn't stop crying.

Finally on the third night I fell into a deep sleep (after a few sleepless nights) and I had an amazing experience. I saw myself back at my childhood home. I was inside where it was clean, tidy and cosy. I was standing at the door looking out into the backyard where, astonishingly, there before me sat Mr Bunny looking his normal, healthy and robust self. However, he had his legs tucked under his body, trying to keep warm because of the atrocious weather! As I looked at the sky it turned various colours from dark grey to blue-grey then almost black – snowing, hailing, torrential rain; violent, blizzard-type weather. And all the while Mr Bunny sat there bearing it all, looking at me with the oddest of expressions as if to say, 'Why are you so upset?'

I couldn't believe what I was seeing and felt that if I left him out there any longer the biting wind would carry him away forever, so I quickly motioned for him to come inside. He stood up and stretched, then slowly hopped toward me, up the steps and into the front door. He put two front feet in the door, looked around, gave a little body shake then happily hopped right inside and I closed the door after him.

I was so happy to have him inside and safe with me. I showed him around and introduced him to the other rabbits (one was a black-and-white rabbit named Charlie, whom I've never heard of … yet).

When I woke I felt absolutely no grief. I felt excited that I had had the chance to see my little friend again whom I absolutely knew without a doubt was now in a happy, loving place. More importantly, he helped me move on. I realized in hindsight the atrocious weather I witnessed was symbolic of my grief and depressive state. This must have been having a terrible effect on Mr Bunny!

I have since dreamt about him twice more. The first time he was lying upside down playfully looking at me. He was sending me the most amazing gushes of love and grati-tude that I have ever experienced in my life. When I woke the next day I knew I had received something very special. The third time he was in the distant background, but still sent me lots of love. I could see that he was well and now moving gradually away towards his new home.

Mr Bunny was so precious and I will never forget him!

CHAPTER 7

Angels from the Afterlife

... without being seen, they are present with you.

Francis de Sales

To many people, their deceased loved ones *are* their angels. Great Grandma is the one who you *feel* comforts you when you are sad, Granddad is the one who 'sits' with you in the car and your late father is always in your heart and protects you at work.

So many lovely stories are based on help and love from our afterlife angels, our loving relatives who have passed into the light. These special loved ones are never forgotten, but there is so much more to it than this.

When we say that our loved ones are close still and watch over us, we mean it literally. It's not just a nice idea. Our relatives and friends who have meant so much to us on this side of life continue to be a part of our lives once they move to their new realm of existence – heaven. They really do still exist. People all over the world see, hear and sense their loved ones *after* they pass on. They appear in special dreams and we feel their reassuring touch – quite literally!

I've written about many of my own experiences in the past and regular readers will be familiar with Eric, my father's late brother, who works with my whole family. Eric flickers lights to let us know he is around, but more importantly he appears to us in dreams to pass on important messages – and sometimes just to say hello.

More recently my late father-in-law has also made several appearances from the other side. Strangely, he visits my sister and passes messages through her – apparently her energy is currently more compatible. But that's just great. Who better to trust than your own sister?

We all like to think that our loved ones exist in another place once we lose them on this side of life, but I *know* that they do. I've already shared hundreds of stories from the other side and, just because there are so many more, I'd love to include a few for you here.

Not Scary at All

John had previously sent me a story about his ex-wife, who'd appeared to him after she passed on. He had seen her sitting on the end of the bed in what is called a 'spirit visitation' experience. That means although he may have been (or appeared to have been) partly asleep, the visit was a real one and not a dream. He felt her appearance was a great reassurance to him and showed him that her consciousness had continued after physical death. Later he wrote to share more experiences:

> It must have been about two years after the death of my granddad and on the day this happened I had not been thinking about him in any way. I got up as usual and when I walked through my bedroom door I smelled cigarette smoke, but strangely, only in the confines of the doorway. As soon as I walked back through, the smell had gone.

John was confused, as you can imagine:

> I walked back in through the door again and it was there again, but only in the doorway. I don't smoke at all and no one had been around my place.

John was unable to investigate further because he had to go to work, but this was far from the end of the story:

> The very next morning, the same thing happened again, and the smell appeared *every day* after that right to the end of the week. I didn't have a clue what it was!

That weekend John was having some friends round:

> The group had decided to get a medium round to do a reading for us all [a medium is a psychic who has the ability to communicate with our loved ones on the other side of

life]. When I had my reading done, the medium told me that there was a thin old man with us and he explained that the man had been a heavy smoker and he used to live next to a cricket field. I knew straight away it was my granddad and realized that Granddad had been bringing me the smoke smell so that I would know he was with me!

Granddad decided to show his presence again:

That night as I lay in bed I felt someone sit on my bed and even felt the mattress go down. I wasn't frightened and just said, 'Hi, Granddad, what's up?'

I began to get pictures in my mind of his old house, then my mum's house (his daughter) and my mum was doing the ironing. Someone told me that this meant there was some unfinished business to take care of.

John felt that he had discovered the reason for the visit:

To cut a long story short, Granddad's son was selling the old house where they had lived for many years and I believe he did not want it sold and wanted it to be kept in the family. Sadly, by the time I realized what it was he wanted, it was too late and the house was sold. I was so sorry that I could not help in time.

John also had a visit from another relative:

Just 12 months ago it was my goddaughter's 21st birthday. Her mum Sue, my good friend, had died of a brain tumour about two years previously. I live in a little cottage in the countryside, so it is a little damp and I have a de-humidifier. On the night of my goddaughter's birthday, I was sleeping and was woken by the sound of my clothes, which I lay on the machine, being thrown onto the floor. To my surprise I heard the wheel of the de-humidifier being turned to 'on' (which is about five turns), then without fail on it came.

John was very surprised by this sound and sat up in bed:

In the room was a beautiful white ball of light and it just hung around the top of the de-humidifier. I knew who it was straight away and just said, 'Hi, Sue, I know why you are here.' At that the light went and I just went right off to sleep!

The next day I rang my goddaughter to tell her that her mum had been to visit, but she already knew. 'She was also here this morning,' she said, and went on to explain how she had been having a shower when the tap in the sink had turned itself on full and the lights had flickered! She also knew right away who it was and we laughed about it and wished Sue all the best in the spirit world.

So you see, spirit contact really is not a scary thing. And although I miss the people who are no longer here, I look at it as if they are just on holiday for a while. I find it very comforting to know I can speak with any of my family or friends and know they will answer me. Pretty cool really.

John's spot on there!

'See You at the Wedding'

One of the sad things about losing a loved one is that we miss them at special family celebrations like weddings and birthday parties. But just because they have crossed to the other side of life, don't believe for one minute that they don't make it to parties! Elaine's mum popped over in a dream to let her know that she'd be there:

> A few months after my mother died I had a dream, but it was really a conversation with her where we were catching up on all the gossip and I was able to share my wedding plans with her. At the end of the conversation, she told me that if she didn't see me before, she would see me on my wedding day!
>
> On the actual day, when we were signing the register we had her favourite piece of music playing, *Ave Maria*, and the sun came through a large stained-glass window at the front of the church right at that point – but it only shone through the depiction of an angel in the glass, not through any other part of the window!
>
> Both my father and I were convinced it was my mum keeping her promise.

Dragonfly

We've already looked at butterfly experiences in the previous chapter, but I thought you might enjoy this dragonfly story too.

Belinda is from England. She told me:

> My nephew died at the age of two-and-a-half weeks, of meningitis. It was very sudden. He left a twin brother. When my sister-in-law used to go and visit him before he was buried, his brother would become very unsettled around the time she was in the funeral home.
>
> My youngest son kept a picture of the twins above his bed, but one night he woke screaming, saying he had felt and seen something red 'whoosh' from above his head and fly out of the window.

Belinda wanted to support her son and bought the book *Waterbugs and Dragonflies* for her children to help them understand about death and the afterlife. 'We found it a beautiful story,' she said, 'and from then on, my nephew's "symbol" was a dragonfly.'

Dragonflies, like butterflies, are regular symbols of eternal life and people do find these creatures around a lot after the loss of a loved one. Belinda found this happened to her:

One day when my sister-in-law and I were cleaning my nephew's grave, a dragonfly appeared, touched her lips, then landed on my shoe!

After that, the dragonfly 'symbol' seemed to start following them around:

We went on holiday to Spain as a family (four adults and seven kids!), and every time we went to the pool, there were two red dragonflies dancing around where we sat!

Every summer since – my nephew would have been five this June – there has been a dragonfly in my garden and several times when we have been sitting in the sun it's landed on my hand for up to a minute a time!

Belinda is aware that it might be possible that we just look for signs anywhere for reassurance and says, 'Of course it could be just a coincidence and us "looking" for a sign, but it has been a source of comfort.'

Whatever you think of it, though, dragonflies just kept popping up for the family:

Every milestone of my nephew's life – walking, first word and starting school – we have seen another little boy doing the same thing right next to him, and every night the kids look at the sky and say good night to 'his' star.

I have been told my eldest has physic abilities, and he has had many dreams of my nephew and other family members who have passed. He also 'saw' people all the time when he was younger, so perhaps this is right.

Happy Mother's Day

Jayne's story is so very sad and tragic:

My daughter Emma-Leigh died in October 2004. She was 17. Emma had been out with friends and had a great fun time. She was found dead later at the bottom of our local mill. I have never found out the full story, only that a young man with mental problems was there that night. He later left a note admitting he was responsible for her death, although he has never verbally admitted it (he is mute), so he was never charged.

I have another daughter, Carla, aged 15, and I am a single mum. As you can imagine my world was completely destroyed after Emma's death, and I can honestly say it still is.

Carla is my strength, but certain days in the calendar are always very hard. On Mother's Day 2005 I was in a terrible state and the night before, in the early hours of the morning, I decided to walk to the mill – what exactly for, I don't know.

When I got to the mill I broke down and just cried and cried. A friend's husband found me and kindly took me back home. As we walked we chatted and I was telling him how I always felt that I'd never got the chance to say goodbye to Emma before she passed away. I wanted so much just to hold and kiss her beautiful face one last time.

The night after Mother's Day I went to bed as usual and had a strange 'dream'. I was in bed and Emma came into my room, but the strange thing was, people were following her. I shot out of bed and pushed them through the door, asking them to leave before I shut the door.

Emma then lay on my bed and I lay beside her and hugged and kissed my daughter. She then started to cry and said, 'I'm so sorry for hurting you, Mum.'

I also cried, and she told me that 'they' had said she could just stop for a brief moment. I asked her if she was OK, to which she replied, 'Yes, Mum, I honestly am.'

I asked what she was doing later and she told me she was clubbing (which she loved to do). When I asked where and she replied something similar to 'Zagazar'. Emma then said that 'they' said because of the suffering I'd been through I was allowed one thing for my house, which seemed a strange thing to say. The girls used to laugh because I always moaned my house wasn't nice enough through lack of funds. I quickly thought about it and said a new stair carpet would be wonderful, because mine needed replacing.

I then asked Emma if she went to her funeral and she replied no, because she hadn't been allowed. I asked if she wanted to see photos of her glass carriage and her face lit up and she said, 'Yes.' I then left the bedroom to get the photographs and to ring her grandparents to let them know she was with me. It was then that I 'woke up'.

The next day I told her granddad about the dream and he told his priest (he's Catholic). The priest explained that it had been a visitation and there was a place in heaven called Xanadu, neither of which I had a clue about!

Some time later I went to Canada to pick up Emma's casket and when I returned my ex-parents-in-law, whom I love very much, had revamped my whole house, including getting me a new stair carpet! It was a wonderful surprise.

Since then Emma has come to me in my dreams many times. She can only stay for a short while each time and I have never had such a strong experience as that first night.

Later I found out that my best friend, my daughter and mum had all prayed for Emma to help me through Mother's Day. I now so believe in the afterlife and know Emma is with us, guiding us until we meet again.

This priest seems to be one of the most enlightened that I have ever heard about. What a wonderful man. I thank him for taking the time to learn about spirit visitation. His response can only help comfort those that are grieving.

Many people write and tell me how they have been comforted by seeing their loved ones in this way. Sadly, when they share this special gift with their religious leaders, they are either told that they are making the experience up or hallucinating or that the experience is evil! What?

However, I know that there are many religious leaders now who are learning about these spiritual experiences so that they can really comment from a place of knowledge – and I thank them for that.

What excites me more than anything is that many spirits now bring the message that 'God' has given them permission to come and visit. Perhaps this will mark a change in our attitude. How can it be wrong to receive spontaneous and loving comfort from the other side of life?

Well, that's my opinion, for what it's worth. So I shall now step down from my soapbox! Ultimately, we all have to decide for ourselves.

Nana Says Goodbye

Just to show you that our loving 'family' of angels visits people of all ages, Nicole is just 11. She is from Ireland and she was lucky enough to receive a comforting visit. She told me, 'When I was five my nana was diagnosed with breast cancer. I was very close to her and didn't understand what people meant when they said she was sick.'

But soon everything was explained in a simple way she could understand:

> One night I had a dream. In it my next-door neighbour rang the doorbell and I ran to answer it. He said, 'Hi, Nicole, I have a special visitor for you, but you have to be quick, as she has a long journey to make.' Then all of a sudden he turned into my nana. She said, 'Nicole, I love you and I always will. Just make sure you remember that, OK? I will be your guardian angel for life.'
>
> I said, 'Nana, I love you too,' and then she had to go, but let me know that one day we would meet again.

Nicole was excited and the next day she ran downstairs to share her experience with her parents. That was when she had the bad news that her nana had passed over, but of course she already knew:

> My parents said, 'Nicole, we have something to tell you.'
>
> I stopped them and said, 'I already know that Nana died last night.'
>
> They were totally stunned, so I told them about the special visit during the night.

I call these dreams 'announcing dreams' and do get a few of them in my postbag. Our loved ones like to say goodbye in a dream if they can, and this was the perfect way for a little girl to understand where her nana had gone. Who better to tell her than her nana herself? This special visit is something that Nicole will treasure for the rest of her life.

Brother Appears on a Bike

Penni is from England and very tragically her brother was killed in a motorbike accident ten years ago. 'He was on holiday in Rhodes when it happened,' she said. 'He he was just 21 years old. We had always been very close, despite our seven-year age gap.'

The young man's death was so unexpected it was a complete shock to the whole family. Penni says:

> I always had the feeling that I had not said goodbye to him properly before he went away. We'd arranged that he would come and see me the day before he went and I was going to lend him some suntan lotions for his holiday, but sadly, our family car had broken down the day before and we had to go and collect it. When he called I wasn't in. He had to go on holiday without the promised lotions and of course I never got to say goodbye. It's funny the things you worry about.
>
> In the days before his funeral I had many thoughts that I wished to share with him. I wanted him to know how much we all loved him and I wanted to say how sorry I was that I had missed the opportunity to say goodbye to him before he left. In fact I was eaten up with guilt about this and so I decided to write a letter to him and place it in his coffin.

Penni suffered terribly, as people do, particularly when there is a young life involved. 'The one thing I wanted in the months that followed,' she said, 'was to dream about him, and try as I might, night after night no dreams came.'

Penni had to wait almost a year after his death, but the dream visitation did come:

> I dreamt I was standing on a roadside at the precise hour and day that he died, but a year further on. In the dream I had the idea that if I could contact him on this day I could stop the accident happening by warning him about it.
>
> Around the corner came my brother riding the motorbike, but not in an upright position – he was sitting astride it as if the bike were lying down on the road, but the wheels were spinning and he was moving towards me. I stepped out into the road and he stopped, got off the bike and walked towards me.

Penni says she thought her plan had worked:

> I thought that I had stopped him from being killed, because he was so clear and lifelike. He hugged me and we walked a little further down the road and stopped outside a small country shop. My brother stood in the doorway of the shop and I remember feeling so elated that he had come back and was alive and well, until an old lady appeared in the doorway also and seemed to pass right through him. It was then that I knew then that I hadn't saved his life and that although he had appeared to me he was still dead.

Her brother sat on some stone steps outside the shop and in his hands he held the letter Penni had written and placed in his coffin:

> He said he wanted to talk to me about it and went through each point in turn, saying he understood why I hadn't been able to say goodbye to him and that it didn't matter about the suntan lotions.

It was just what Penni needed to hear so that she could move on in her life.

> We ended the meeting with him telling me he was proud of me, and I told him the same thing and we then told each other how much we loved each other and had a final hug before he said he now had to go. He got back on the bike and just rode away, and this is where the dream ended.

When Penni woke up she had a feeling of intense well-being, as though the visit had been real. There were also lasting effects:

> Afterwards I stopped feeling so guilty about not saying goodbye because I felt that I'd had another chance to do so.
>
> I can remember this experience very clearly, because I have replayed it in my mind so many times. Remembering it always gives me some comfort. I like to think that my brother had come to help me come to terms with his death.

So many people feel guilty about not being able to say goodbye, but of course it's impossible to be with every single family member when they pass over. It's just the natural order of things and no one's fault. Never feel bad about this or blame yourself. Your loved ones understand and won't blame you in any way.

'Mum Lets Us Know She Is There'

Jenna, from England, also had a sudden loss: 'My mum died unexpectedly and we were all very shocked, but despite that I am convinced that she is showing us she is still around.'

After Jenna's mother died the family began to experience a lot of paranormal phenomena. Jenna told me:

> I was in my dad's house with my two young children and at the time I was washing the dishes. Suddenly the lights started flickering in the kitchen and in the living room where my dad was sitting, but for some reason the lights in the middle room were just fine.
>
> I went into the living room to talk to my dad about the lights and he told me had said out loud, 'Is that you, love?' and the lights had flickered even more strongly.

Her young children seem aware of the visitor too:

My two daughters are three and two and have both been visited by my mum. My three year old woke up once shortly after my mum's death and said, 'Nana came to see me last night and said that she loved me.'

Then on another occasion, my two year old was watching TV with me and out of the blue said, 'There's Nanny over there!' I asked her where and she pointed and got quite annoyed at me when she realized that I couldn't see her too!

It seems that Jenna's mother is never too far away:

She often visits me in my dreams and once asked, 'Is it February there?' I later found out that they don't have the same frame of reference for time in the spirit world. I love it that my mum lets us know that she is still very much around and certainly not gone.

A Dream Visit from Italian 'Nonna'

Dee's grandmother is Italian and her passing is quite recent. Dee told me:

Understandably I was devastated. She didn't have a very pleasant ending to her life and for some time afterwards I felt awful because I wish I had done more to help her in her final days. However, I have since got over this feeling a bit because my family have told me I did everything I could and there was no way to get rid of her pain altogether.

Dee's worry is similar to that of so many people who write to me. She said:

I just hated seeing my glamorous and wonderful Nonna like that, as if all her energy had been taken away. She had a personality and a half and a typical Italian 'stubborn' streak! I admired her and respected her so much.

It seems that Nonna's old self returned on the spirit side of life, however, and she was soon back for a visit:

The night that Nonna died, I had a really vivid dream about her. We were on a train in Italy and she was going to show me round and introduce me to other family members out there that I'd never met. She looked younger again, more like how she looked when I was a child. She was wearing a dress that I have seen her wearing in a photo. It was a strange coincidence in a way, because this was a journey that my brother had made with Nonna many years ago, but I never got to go at the time.

Clearly Nonna didn't want Dee to feel left out!

Dee went on to say, 'She was happy and relaxed in the dream, and didn't really say much. I had similar dreams about her almost nightly for quite some time after her death.'

Dee explained that there had been quite a lot of problems with the family and because of this there was quite a long period of time between Nonna's cremation and her ashes actually being put into the ground. 'During this time I would dream about her so often,' she told me, 'and the dreams made me feel as though I hadn't been to sleep. I was really tired every day.'

Everything seemed to change after the ashes had been laid to rest, though:

> Once we had buried her ashes the dreams stopped completely. I just shrugged it off as coincidence. When she first died I had a lot of involvement with sorting out the funeral, etc. – I even took time off work to do this, which is unlike me – and then after that my dad was responsible for sorting out the ashes. So I thought that perhaps I was having these dreams because I'd failed to complete her send-off. Maybe they'd stopped because my mind was now at peace, or maybe it was because she was.

After this Dee did have one further dream, though:

> I dreamed that my partner and I were in bed at home and I was aware of lots of spirits around us. I was really afraid. Then we heard the shower 'click' on, and I told my partner to go and see who was in there. Then I heard Nonna, in her

usual strong Italian accent, say, 'Paul, make Nonna a cup of tea!' It was at this point that I woke up, shouting 'Make the spirits go away!' in my sleep!

It sounds crazy, and OK, maybe I had eaten something strange before I went to bed, but it felt so real and I was genuinely scared. I am a bit worried now that I have frightened my Nonna away and I didn't mean to!

I laughed when I read this part of Dee's story, because so many people long for a sign from their loved ones but at the same time are terrified that they might actually visit. Remember that the love we shared with them on this side of life continues on the other. Your dear grandmother is simply *not* going to hurt you!

Dee knows that her visits were a blessing and it was wonderful to see Nonna looking so well on the other side.

Lots of Visits, Lots of Love

Marie was 20 years old when she had the first of many visitation experiences:

The first experience is so vivid still, even though it happened many years ago. It must have been a Saturday, as my husband was at work and I was busy doing the housework (as usual). I was vacuuming our lounge and singing along to the music I was playing, just to get through the boredom!

> The next thing that happened was I remember just stopping what I was doing. The vacuum was still switched on but I was literally frozen to the spot. I felt the strong sensation that somebody was behind me!
>
> It all happened so quickly – one minute I was vacuuming and singing and then the atmosphere around me just changed and I felt compelled to stop what I was doing. I was close to the front door and hallway of our house and I remember distinctly thinking that it couldn't be my husband (who had a regular habit of creeping up behind me and making me jump!), as he was at work and I had not heard his keys in the door.

These 'frozen to the spot' experiences are a common theme and you will find other examples in the book.

Marie continues:

> The next thing I felt was quite a warm feeling on the back of my neck (just below my left ear), as if someone was behind me but close enough for me to feel their breath on my neck. As I tried to rationalize the experience, this 'someone' whispered my name right into my left ear!
>
> As you can imagine, I switched the vacuum off immediately and just shot back into the chair behind me, yelling out, 'Who's there?' but of course there was nobody there. I remember shaking and feeling uneasy because of the shock, but I also knew that it was somebody's way of introducing themselves to me!

Later Marie thought she might have discovered the visitor's name:

> I have since been told that it was my husband's brother, who passed away at the age of 19, coming to say hello to me. My husband said he had a great sense of humour and I guess it was his way of teasing me as my husband did!

Then Marie had another experience, again with her husband's family:

> Since my husband's Aunt Betty passed away from leukaemia in 2005 I have had a few experiences which I know are real. Even though she was my husband's relative, I was very close to her and regularly visited her with our two children.

A dream visit came shortly after her passing:

> This was no ordinary dream, though it is hard to describe to anybody why it felt so real. I remember feeling that I was standing at the top of our stairs and seeing my husband's aunt's face as clear as anything! She had a radiant smile and looked in perfect health and so contented. I remember her saying to me in a lovely soft manner, 'It's OK. I'm OK. I'm happy now.' I felt very comforted by this and knew it was her way of letting me and the rest of the family know that she was at peace.

I did question whether this could have been just a dream, but it was too powerful an image and too strong a feeling. I can't explain how it felt, but it eased some of my pain!

Then Betty came again:

A short while after this I had another 'dream' visit. At this particular time I was still struggling to cope with my grief and was spending a lot of time worrying. In the dream I was sitting somewhere beautiful and peaceful on a bench with Betty by my side. She was holding my hand and we just seemed to sit there for ages, not speaking. I remember saying to her after a while, 'But I thought you had gone.'

Betty replied, 'I have, but I have just come back to see you and then I am going again.' It was all very matter of fact, as if she had just popped back to see me.

Questioning like this is common. Many people who see loved ones in dream visits say, 'But you're dead, aren't you?' or something similar.

Betty continued to hold Marie's hand for a while in reassurance:

This was typical of my husband's aunt, as she was a quiet and private person of very few words and she was very wise, kind and reassuring in nature. Again, I knew that this was more than just a dream and I believe she came to me right when I needed her.

Another strange experience happened to Marie a short while later:

I saw something at night that helped convince me that there is life after death and that I must be open to the other side. People may say that this is not proof to them, but I know I was shown this 'something' or 'someone' to prove it to me, as I had been questioning whether I had been having ordinary dreams or actual visitations.

The experience happened in the middle of the night:

It was dark and I was sleeping on my back when for some reason I woke suddenly, almost in a panic, as if somebody had woken me up quickly! I don't remember hearing anything at all, but opened my eyes quickly and felt my heart beating fast. I don't know why or how, but I felt the strangest of sensations – I literally felt that I was being pulled up into a sitting position in bed. I can't say I felt the need to sit up at that particular moment, because I'm not keen on the dark, but it was a slow, flowing, graceful movement, as if I was being guided up for a reason.

Marie felt compelled to look across the landing and wondered if one of her children had got up to use the bathroom. Maybe this was why she had woken up?

> I couldn't hear anything at all, but just knew to look in that direction. It is quite difficult to describe exactly what I saw next, but I remember seeing something bright and white, almost like a mist, flash past from the bathroom towards our daughter's bedroom. It had no definite outline and was about 5ft tall. I distinctly remember it being bright and white, not quite a mist but a little more definite. The speed was what was most memorable, because it moved so quickly.
>
> The strange thing was that I didn't feel at all frightened. I felt very contented and just smiled to myself, thinking that it was my husband's aunt coming to check on us and our children.

Marie didn't trust her vision completely, though, so followed up:

> I checked with my daughter the next morning to see if she had got up in the night and she said she hadn't. Then I realized she was wearing the brightest pink and lilac pajamas you can imagine, so it clearly hadn't been her!
>
> I sincerely believe our loved ones are with us, particularly in times when we are in distress and really need to call upon them.

One Last Special Smile

Jeanette wrote to tell me that her brother had passed on after four years of suffering and going in and out of hospital. He had been just 34 years old. 'It broke my heart,' she said, 'and I couldn't stop worrying about him, wondering if he was OK or if he was on his own and where he was.'

Jeanette's family went on holiday a few weeks later. She told me:

> It was a mistake, because my brother was supposed to be there with us. I missed him even more, but the strange thing was that everywhere we went we heard the record that we had played at his funeral and in the end I broke down in a restaurant when we walked in and they started playing that record.

It's likely that the song was playing on purpose. It's amazing how much power our loved ones on the other side have with such things!

Jeanette continued, 'My husband tried to comfort me and I told him I just needed to know my brother was OK.'

Maybe 'someone' was listening to the request, because Jeanette got her wish that very night:

> I had a dream that I walked through some doors and there in the room was a single bed with what looked like a matron of the ward. It was quite a big ward, but as I said, there was only one bed in it. The matron was standing next to the bed and my brother was in it, sitting up smiling. He told me that he was OK now and free from pain and that I wasn't to worry anymore.
>
> When I woke the next day I told my husband about my dream and he thought that my brother had come to let me know how he was. I agreed, because it was so real and I felt such relief the next day. I just can't explain it, but I do believe my brother came to me because we were close and he would worry about me all the time when he was here.

Just to be sure, Jeanette's brother also visited his other sister:

> My sister said he visited her as well. When she woke up he was sitting at the bottom of her bed. She told me he smiled at her and then left, but she said she felt so much better for it.

He's been dead nearly ten years now and I've never dreamed about him since, but I know he's around, I just feel it!

A Telephone Visit

Melanie is from England and I thought her story really illustrated how hard our loved ones work to make us feel secure in our experiences. If they can bring in something which feels familiar to us then they certainly will.

Melanie told me:

> I was going through a traumatic time in my life. My boyfriend was due in court, I had temporarily moved in with my sister and was trying to get a place for myself and my children to live in and my ex-husband was being very elusive.

Melanie's life was certainly complicated and it is at these times that we need the most reassurance from our loved ones. Melanie was at breaking-point:

> I didn't know if I could get my children's possessions back from my ex-husband's house or even if he was still going to see the children. It doesn't sound much, but it was my crisis and I was worried sick and hadn't been sleeping very well.

We often feel that we have to deal with our problems alone, but that's not true. Even if we seem to be alone, our angels and loved ones on the other side will be keeping an eye on us and sometimes have the ability to see a little way ahead in our life. They're not really meant to give too much away, but sometimes a little information helps our sanity!

Melanie had a strange experience she will never forget:

> One night I dreamed of a phone ringing. It woke me up and, thinking it was the real phone, I picked it up and said, 'Hello.'
>
> My nan, who had died in 1976, said, 'It's Nanny.'
>
> I was totally taken off guard and said, 'Who?'
>
> 'It's Nanny. Everything's going to be OK,' she replied.

What a wonderful experience! Her nan had chosen to visit Melanie and give her the reassurance that she so badly needed at that time. She told me, 'I hadn't heard her voice since I was a teenager, but it was most definitely her, and I felt so peaceful and knew that everything would work out right, as it did.'

I have heard before of loved ones from the other side of life 'telephoning' in dreams. Yes! I've read several similar stories and I love them all.

'Well Now'

Here is another story where a loved one sends that all-important message to say that after passing they have regained full health. Morgan is also from England. Here is her story.

In November 2006 my younger cousin Kimberley passed away in her sleep after living with leukaemia for four years of her life. Four of us had always hung around together – my sister and I and our two cousins. We were inseparable and always up to mischief. Although we grew apart early in our teens, we began to grow closer once Kimberley turned 18 and I turned 20.

Kimberley's death brought a great amount of grief to my family and then just five months later my grandmother also crossed over. We like to think they are together and it does bring us some comfort.

I had never had a firm belief about what might happen to us after death, although my cousin's parting made me think about this more. A week after her funeral I had a vivid dream about her. My cousin and I were standing together in a plain white glowing setting. There were no features around either of us that I can remember, and Kimberley was asking me how everyone was and how everyone was feeling. I got confused and kept telling her she was dead so she couldn't ask me this. This made Kimberley laugh and I woke up.

Here again the dreamer says, 'But you're dead, aren't you?' or a similar phrase. That's what makes the experience a visitation and not an ordinary dream – we know that the person is no longer living on the Earth plane and we are aware and lucid in the dream.

Morgan continued:

As I woke up I could still hear Kimberley's voice, and I can still see her in this dream, wearing brown, which was her favourite colour. Her clothes looked like the ones we had buried her in! I personally believe, as do my family, that she was visiting us and reassuring us that she was fine and well and happy.

Then she visited me again in a dream. I remember my sister and cousin and I were having a sleepover at the time, like we did as children. I remember getting the sense that we probably wouldn't hear from Kimberley again after that, that this sleepover was the last chance we would get to do so, but since then I have had the sense of her *being* in dreams, though I cannot quite remember them the next morning now, and I still sense her around me.

About six weeks after my cousin's death, my grandmother fell into a deep sleep following a stroke. For 10 weeks her frail self fought on, never moving, waking or sleeping and all the time growing weaker, until she passed one night in her sleep. We believe she was giving our family time to recover from the death of our cousin, because a second death so soon would have been heartbreaking for us.

Before she passed, my grandmother suffered from really bad arthritis, to the point where she couldn't move and could hardly speak or eat. Though strangely, four days before she had her stroke, my mother was visiting her and she suddenly announced in a very clear voice, 'Kimberley's better now. She's all better now.' We were stunned, because we had never told her about my cousin's death, as she was too ill herself.

Gran never spoke again after this, so we firmly believe that Kimberley had visited her to let us all know that she was at peace and cured of the cancer in her new home.

Soul Mates

Denise wrote to me from Australia and had several stories to share:

My nana passed away a few years ago. All that morning I felt that something was wrong and I just could not put my finger on it. It turned out that my nana had been taken to hospital and later that day my dad called to say that she was crashing and we were to go straight to the hospital. My husband drove and I just sat there crying, I was so upset.

All of a sudden a feeling of warmth and calmness came over me and I was not upset anymore and stopped crying. I felt that everything was OK. Just at that moment I looked at my watch. Why? I have no idea, but the time was 6:01 p.m.

When we got to the hospital and to my nana's room she had already passed over. The attending doctor said that she had passed at 6:01 p.m. and I knew then that Nana had let me know that she was at peace.

A few months later I had to have emergency surgery for a ruptured cyst in my ovaries. I was bleeding internally.

During the surgery I saw a bright light and my nana was right in the middle of it. It was as if I was looking at a real person. She reached her hand to me and hugged me. Again I felt a sense of warmth and comfort and wasn't scared anymore. She told me that I was going to be OK and that she was there to watch over me, which was wonderful.

When I woke up from the surgery I wanted to tell my husband and parents, then I decided not to because I was afraid they would think I was nuts! I've read a lot about these types of experiences now and realize they are quite common.

'Arrived Safely'

Bernadette Hunt is from England and has had many experiences:

From a very early age I have seen and dreamed about different spirits. Then after the birth of my third child and the death of my grandmother and father, paranormal things seemed to happen on a more regular basis.

One of the most vivid experiences took place a few days after my father died. I had not quite fallen asleep one night when I felt an overwhelming feeling of warmth and calm and then I saw my grandmother. She said that my father had arrived safely and had met Karen. As she moved away, I saw my father sitting in a park area with a young woman kneeling next to him. I didn't know who Karen was, but my grandmother just said, 'They named her Karen.'

The day before my father's funeral I asked my mother if she had lost any children that I didn't know about. She was quite shocked that I had asked her this and told me she had miscarried a child between me and my youngest brother (I have three brothers and three sisters). It had never been discussed because she had found the whole thing very traumatic. So I took a rose to my father's funeral for Karen too.

My youngest daughter also seems to be very psychic. She was very matter of fact when my father died, although she was only five at the time. She told me that he was OK now, as if she had some higher information about the whole thing. She also pointed out my grandmother in a photograph but was unaware that Grandma had worn glasses. Apparently the spirit of my late grandmother had been visiting her and told her that God had made Grandma's eyes better when she died.

Loving Family Members Who Have Never Really Gone at All …

Sarah has experienced so much tragedy in her life that her story made me cry but then smile because her loved ones had a way of showing they were still around her.

Sarah had so many experiences it was hard to decide what to tell you. In the end I decided to give you almost all of her story, even though it's a long one. She wrote:

When I was very little, I had several 'experiences'. I frequently had vivid, colourful dreams of flying and being able to watch myself asleep in bed, as if I were out of my body. I thought they were the most beautiful dreams and so lifelike!

When I was eight, my older sister, who was 17, was killed in a tragic car crash. It was so awful. A few weeks before the crash she had been having a conversation with my mum and had informed her that she would be killed in a crash and that Mum was to look after her new kitten. It was as if she had predicted this awful experience. Sadly, the kitten was killed on the road in front of our house six weeks before Jayne herself was taken. Then, very strangely, six weeks *after* Jayne died, a cat identical to my sister's (that we had buried), appeared on the doorstep and refused to leave us!

As a child, I constantly heard my name being called when no one was around. Mum always said it was Jayne communicating and I liked to believe it was.

A couple of years after my sister died, my grandmother died too. She was very old and I can only ever remember her after she had a major stroke which left her severely disabled, unable to talk or walk and completely paralysed down her right side.

One night I was lying in bed, facing away from the door, when I heard the door open. My eyes were open and I remember clearly seeing a shaft of light fill the room. The door closed again and there was a bump on my bed. I remember assuming that Mum had let the cat in (the one that had adopted us), but when I sat up, there was an indentation on the bed but no cat. The experience had been so real that I searched the room, but found nothing.

Then I heard Grandma's voice, which was strange because, as I said, I had no recollection of her ever being able to talk and I was only a babe in arms when she had the stroke, but somehow I knew this was Grandma. I wasn't frightened, but comforted. She seemed to be telling me that she was looking after me and was with me. I told Mum the next morning and she didn't seem surprised that Grandma had visited me, saying that she had always loved me and wanted to comfort me, especially now Jayne had gone too. It made sense.

I met my future husband when I was 14 years old. I had only been seeing him a couple of months when it was New Year's Eve. Mum and Dad decided to go out and left us alone for the evening. Just after midnight, Mum rang and said they were on their way home, so my boyfriend started to put on his hat and scarf ready to go, looking into the mirror as he did so. Now, he has always been a self-proclaimed cynic when it comes to anything paranormal. He believes in the 'here and now', black and white and little else! However, I can remember vividly the look on his face as he looked into the mirror and then shot around quickly, staring at the chair in the corner. I asked him what was the matter, but he just shook his head and said, 'Nothing.'

Years later, he confessed what he'd seen. As he'd looked into the mirror, he'd seen a very young woman sitting in the chair. Not believing his eyes, he'd turned quickly and looked at the chair, assuming the image would disappear – but it didn't! He told me the teenager had long dark hair and was dressed in a white and pink bridesmaid's dress. He said he could see her so clearly it was as if she were actually in the room with us. She smiled at him and put up her hand and said, 'Hello.' Then she was gone. He didn't feel he could tell me at the time because I'd only been seeing him a couple of months and he was afraid I'd think he was barmy!

When he finally did tell me, I rushed to the old box of photos I'd been given when Mum and Dad had passed. I knew exactly the photograph I was looking for. Finding the one I wanted, I showed it to him. It was Jayne in the pink and white bridesmaid's dress she'd worn for my uncle's wedding some three or four years before her death. The chair she was sitting in was one that Mum affectionately called 'Jayne's chair', as it was her favourite to snuggle up in. My husband said he had felt at the time that she was giving him her approval. How I wished he'd had the courage to tell me then because I know it would have been a great comfort to us all.

Unfortunately, my life has been plagued by unhappy events. Although I had a very secure, privileged, loving upbringing, my lovely family was all taken away from me suddenly, one by one. My mum passed suddenly when I was only 19, just before my wedding. I was devastated beyond belief and can honestly say that now, some 18 years later, I am still grieving and miss her so much.

Just before my wedding, I hit rock bottom. I so wanted Mum to be there. Luckily, I still had my dad, but of course we all felt that something was missing. Then one night, I had a dream. Again, this was unusually real and vivid. It was my wedding day and everything was exactly as it actually was going to be on the actual day; every little detail, even my dress. The only thing was that everyone was crying. I was walking down the aisle with Dad and on both sides everyone was sobbing. When I reached the front, I looked back to give my bridesmaid my flowers and that was when I saw Mum sitting in the front pew talking to an older grey-haired lady. I'm still unsure whether this was my grandma (her mum) or my other gran, who had died a couple of years earlier. As I looked at Mum, she turned to me and gave me a brilliant loving smile saying, 'Why are they all crying? I'm here, aren't I?'

I immediately woke up, but felt strangely calm. I knew in my heart that Mum would be at my wedding. It was such a comfort to know that and it got me through the day with a smile on my face.

Then, just after my wedding, my world shattered again. Police came to tell me that Dad had died suddenly of a heart attack whilst driving his car. He loved driving and would frequently take the long way round. 'Why do one mile when you can do ten?' he would joke. He drove around the country a lot after Mum went. He missed her so terribly. The day of his funeral, he made us smile. It should have been a very short route to the crematorium, but instead the journey took over half an hour. The hearse driver took such a long route that we ended up driving all through the countryside! Even my sceptical brother commented that it was typical of Dad to go the long way round and not straight there!

Mum and Dad have brought me such comfort since they passed, though, and there are always little things that show they are around. When they died, I inherited a dinner service. I never actually used it much, preferring to keep it for best. A few items needed replacing and I only knew of one outlet that still sold the dinner service. I rang the supplier and was told to my dismay that although they did do a pattern that was very similar, they no could no longer obtain the original design. I was very upset.

A few nights later I was talking to Mum in a dream again. She came to me and I explained to her that I wanted to use the dinner service but I couldn't replace the marked or chipped items because I could not get the same pattern. Mum told me not to worry. She explained, 'If you take a look at the newer cups, you will see that the pattern is different from the plates, etc., but it's not *too* bad, it's nearly alike.' Again, this dream was very vivid and I even woke crying and felt really emotional again.

Later that day, I remembered Mum's words and dug out the service from the back of the dresser. Finding the cups, I unwrapped them from their bubble wrap and then did the same with the plates. Sure enough, Mum was right. The pattern on the cups was different, but similar enough to pass as the set! I went and replaced the missing pieces and still happily use them to this day.

Other strange things have happened over the years. On the fifth anniversary of my dad's passing, I was in the lounge with my little boy when we heard a strange noise. A blackbird came down the chimney, covering the room with soot. That evening, as we took up the ruined carpet, we laughed and said it was Dad popping in to say hello.

Then this November, the fifteenth anniversary of Dad's death, I was telling someone at work that it was the anniversary and suddenly the lights flickered. My friend laughed and said, 'Perhaps that's your Dad letting you know he is still with you.' I laughed, but felt strangely comforted, and delighted in relaying the event half an hour later to another colleague. As if by magic, as I was telling her what had happened, the lights flickered again!

This is truly a sign you may say, but the day got stranger. After work, I collected the children from school and went home. On opening the lounge door, what should appear but another blackbird that had come down the chimney, ten years to the day on Dad's anniversary!

Other events have happened in my life too, some of which I am still unable to fathom. Not long after my husband and I moved into our second home we were watching a new TV comedy show about a Jewish ghost. As we lay in bed later that evening we were laughing about it and saying how funny it would be if we had our own ghost. At that very moment, the cupboard door creaked open a few inches! We laughed and my husband got out of bed and shut it tightly, even pulling the handle to ensure it wouldn't open again. He got back into bed and within a minute it opened again!

Feeling a little spooked, we decided to leave it open and turned off the light to settle down. Literally two minutes later the smoke alarm started to bleep erratically. My husband went and checked everywhere, but there was nothing that could have set the alarm off, so he got into bed and turned off the light again. Almost immediately, the smoke alarm bleeped erratically again. My husband then decided enough was enough, so went and took the battery out. But, yes, you've guessed it! It went off again – this time without the battery. We were really freaked out by this time and said aloud, 'Whoever this is, please leave us to get some sleep.' We turned off the light and settled down for a peaceful night.

The next morning we were discussing these two events in the kitchen. Suddenly the hot tap started to gush with water at high speed. My husband stood by the sink desperately trying to turn off the tap, but it wouldn't budge either way. It was completely jammed and hot water was rushing everywhere. He stepped back so he could look under the sink for his tools and that's when the water stopped, as quickly as it had begun!

Now we were a little scared and decided to go out for the day to take our minds off what was fast becoming very 'unreal!' We decided we would go around the shops to get ideas for decorating our new home. We made our purchases and decided the next day, Sunday, we would make a start on decorating the hall, stairway and landing.

There was a large handrail going all the way up the stairs and across the top onto the landing. I couldn't make up my mind whether or not I wanted to keep this. My husband was unscrewing it from the wall so as to make decorating a little easier. When he got to the last bit across the top, the screws wouldn't budge and I had still not made up my mind. My husband was starting to get exasperated, both with me and the stubborn screws, and said to me, 'Make up your mind, because I'm going to have to smash this piece to get it off if you don't want it. If you do, I won't remove it.'

I made a snap decision and said, 'Smash it off. I hate it and don't want to keep it.'

No sooner had I finished saying the sentence than the piece of wood simply fell off the wall! Underneath was written: 'PUT IT BACK!'

After the freaky weekend we'd had, we didn't need telling further. The decorating was finished and the handrail put back.

Recently I was feeling sorry for myself and had been crying. I sat on the bed and said aloud, 'Please, Mum, Dad, Jayne, if you can hear me, if you are with me, please,

please give me some sign so I know.' I said this every day for over a week, but no signs presented themselves and I sank lower and lower.

Then one night I had a dream and again it was vivid, colourful and lifelike. Mum, Dad and Jayne were all there, as well as others that at the time I couldn't place or see clearly. They were just hazy figures, but somehow I knew that I knew them. They were all doing silly things – Jayne was juggling, Mum was throwing cuddly toys around and Dad was moving stuff around. I questioned what they were doing, feeling really puzzled, and then the message was really clear. Dad said, 'Look, love, we're here for you. We always are and always have been. We love you and will never leave you. We don't have to do silly tricks to show you. Trust us and believe in us. We love you.'

I woke up crying and the air was thick and heavy with emotion, but I think I had my answer.

If you haven't had an experience relating to a loved one on the other side, don't feel you are missing out. Just remember Sarah's dad's message to us all: 'We're here for you. We always are and always have been … we don't have to do silly tricks to show you.' He has a point!

CHAPTER 8

Angels and Miracles – and Some Fun Stories Too!

Miracles are not contrary to nature,
but only contrary to what we know about nature.

Saint Augustine

I guess in many ways you could say that every visit from an angel is a miracle. We've looked at stories involving great drama and lifesaving achievements and also know that angels appear when we are sad, stressed and grieving. Sometimes they come to us when we need to change direction or to show us that we are on the right path after all.

Angels also appear to collect our loved ones when it's 'their time' and are around when new loved ones are born. Sometimes they like to appear just to show us that they are around. They want us to acknowledge their presence in our lives and give them permission to help. Remember, angels have to be asked if we want them to guide us.

Angels in Our Lives

Let's have a look at some of the little everyday things our angels do.

Angel Batteries

Angela is from England. She told me:

> I asked my angel to show me they were around and then I found a large white feather on the floor of my bedroom. My husband tried to find a logical reason for it, but I was convinced it was the first sign from my angel.
>
> This morning I was walking to work when my MP3 player battery ran out. Without thinking, I started talking to my angels, as I do when I am alone. I asked them if they could please send me a battery for my MP3 player. I said, 'It doesn't have to be a new one, I need just enough power to get me to work, as I enjoy listening to music on the way to work.'

Angela says that she was a little impatient as she was looking for a battery:

> Then I said quietly, 'Sorry, angels, the request is not for a greater good,' and I felt a little guilty for troubling them with such a menial request. However, as I finished saying the sentence, I noticed right next to my left foot there was a very

rusty AAA battery, which was all I needed for my MP3 player.

Angela said it was a good job no one was around because she started laughing to herself:

The condition of the battery was so bad it looked as though it wouldn't work (it was very battered and rusty). But I couldn't leave it there because it is what I had asked for and my request had been answered. So, while still chuckling to myself, I picked it up and replaced the one from my player with it. At first it didn't work, so I took it back out and scraped some of the rust off each end and put it back in!

She was stunned when the player began to work:

I was able to play my MP3 player for another 15 minutes. I couldn't stop smiling, knowing my angels had answered my request.

Then, as I got to the car park at work, the battery completely died. This was amazing, because I had actually said I just needed enough power to get me to work. They had given me exactly what I had asked for.

Angela made sure to thank her angels. She said:

I know without a doubt they were with me and answered my request. I have told special friends at work what happened, but I haven't told my husband. He'll probably try and explain it away with logic!

'Angels Helped Me All Day'

Lisa's story is a fun one because she decided to 'test' her angels to see if they were working with her. I'll let Lisa herself describe the results:

Yesterday I decided that I would meditate and ask the angels for some help with a few things that were troubling me. After a short while I began to feel a bit silly, so gave up, but not before I had asked them some questions.

Afterwards I was bored and was just daydreaming. I thought to myself, 'I wish that something good would happen,' and within a second of that thought the phone rang and it was a company offering me a job interview. This might not mean anything to some people, but it was actually one of the things I had requested in my meditation just moments before!

In the late afternoon I set off to pick up my children from school. I had been dreading the mayhem that comes with all of the necessary parenting activities. I think that all parents at some stage feel at their wits' end due to one thing or another and I had been feeling a little overwhelmed by my children's behaviour.

During my meditation I had asked my angels if there was any way that they could help me to calm the boys down a little. I was stunned when one of my sons gave me a letter from the school advising me that they were all to take part in a new initiative to encourage the social, emotional and behavioural development of the children. The school had decided it would make the place a friendlier environment to work in if they concentrated on the children's behaviour. I couldn't have agreed more! That week the 'whole school goal' was to talk calmly and quietly to each other. It was an answered prayer!

I was excited and talked to my husband Mike about the things I had asked my angels to help me with during the day. Needless to say, he was quite sceptical, but I told him that I had requested help with one more thing but that I wouldn't tell him what it was because it involved Mike himself. I wasn't sure if the angels could intervene on another's behalf, but I had decided to go ahead and ask them just in case.

I'd become worried because Mike and his brother had argued and neither of them had made any effort to heal the rift between them. Mike's brother wanted an apology from Mike, but because Mike felt that he wasn't in the wrong he'd decided it just wasn't going to happen. They were both being stubborn and it was such a silly thing. I had asked my angels to bring them closer again and help them to forgive each other. I know it was a lot to ask.

By now it was late in the evening and I was trying to think of a way that I might be able to get the brothers together. Whilst I was doing this, the phone rang. It was

Mike's brother and he had telephoned to tell Mike that his fiancée was pregnant with twins! Of course the news was so exciting that they both forgot about the argument. I was overjoyed!

I explained to my husband that my third request had been that he and his brother make up again. This time even Mike was stunned. We both concluded that we had received proof that angels do exist!

Open House

Wendy is from Belgium. Her life seems to walk hand in hand with the paranormal and she's had several experiences of afterlife contact. I'll let her explain:

I'm 32 years old and have had several encounters and messages from beyond. The experiences seem to happen most at times when I need a little reassurance in my life.

The first time I had such an experience was two years ago. I'd lost a close family member and I was so overwhelmed with grief that I asked all of the people I knew who had crossed over to let me know if they were OK and happy. To be honest, I didn't expect to receive any reaction, but after a few minutes I heard very clearly the sound of an angel choir! It was so nice, soft, calming and soothing that I immediately felt comforted and relieved.

My uncle had died from cancer and I was sad that I hadn't had the opportunity to say goodbye, so found it hard to let him go. One night he appeared to me in a type of dream. He was lying on the sofa, surrounded by the family and my aunt, his wife. He asked me if I now felt able to let him go. I said, 'Yes,' rather reluctantly, but of course I took great comfort in knowing he wasn't alone. My aunt was smiling and she thanked me and took my uncle with her, and as he went he turned from a very sick old-looking man to a young vibrant man, full of life. I was so shocked I woke up, sitting straight up in bed. But I was happy.

Then in 2003, a few months before the birth of my second child, I woke up around 3 a.m. to see a man standing next to my bed. I didn't feel scared as he put his hand on my belly and said, 'It's alright. I'm here now.' It appeared to be my son's guardian angel just keeping an eye on him before he was born. The angel was a young man wearing a black shirt and a hard-rock type of necklace. I couldn't see his face very clearly, but I knew he was floating – I couldn't see his feet and it was as if he had none.

At the end of 2004, I was feeling worried about my family. We'd had some health issues with the children and I was concerned about them. In the middle of the night I woke up to the very strong smell of cigars. No one at home smokes cigars and we hadn't had any visitors who were cigar smokers that I knew of. I slowly opened my eyes and there he was: a man with a very long beard, dressed in a brown cloak with a cord round his waist, smoking a cigar. Before I could ask who he was, he told me the kids were fine and I didn't need to worry. And he vanished right in front of me! Another guardian angel, I guess.

Then one morning a few weeks back I was in the kitchen preparing the kids' meal when I saw a little white angel floating by the kitchen door in the direction of the living room. I immediately put on the light in the living room, but she had gone. I was sad because I thought I had scared her away.

Now, though, I've discovered she is always around me: on the radio in the kitchen (her favourite place to hang out) and even *in* the radio (singing the first words of a song *before* the lyrics begin). She teases my dog; she makes the doorbell go and the phone ring. I haven't noticed my kids or my partner seeing or hearing her, but I know she's here. And when I asked how I could make my sceptical partner accept the fact that I had seen an angel, that night I found a white feather in the dryer – her way of showing my partner I'm not going crazy.

A Missing Lighter

OK, to be fair a missing lighter is not really a miracle story, but I just had to include it here.

Dave told me:

Four years ago my mother passed to the spirit world after a battle with lung cancer. The morning of the funeral was a bit hectic, running people around in the car, picking up flowers and so on. When I had five minutes to spare I parked the car and decided to have a cigarette. I went into the front room of our house and put my tobacco pouch and lighter on the couch, then just popped to the toilet. When I came back I went to roll a cigarette but noticed the lighter had gone. I looked all around the couch, under the cushions, everywhere, but it was nowhere to be found.

I thought I might have made a mistake and left the lighter in the car, so popped out to the car and had a search around, but still no lighter. We had some spare lighters in a drawer, so I didn't worry about it too much at the time, even though I was convinced I had left it on top of my tobacco pouch!

Imagine my shock then when I got back to the couch and looked down at my pouch: there was my lighter sitting right on top of it. My wife was the only other person in the house and she was upstairs at the time. I thought she must have come down whilst I was looking in the car and found it, so I asked her where she'd found my lighter, but she hadn't been downstairs and hadn't even realized that I had been back in the house.

When I sat down and thought about it, I realized that my mother had made this happen to let me know she was around but also to warn me to give up the cigarettes. I'm pleased to report that I did give them up just six months later.

Actually, maybe this is a miracle story after all!

Angel 'Spirits'

Angie's story is a lot of fun and you can feel her lovely upbeat energy in her account:

You may think this completely unbelievable and that I have absolutely the silliest thoughts in my head, but my story is totally true.

We sold our farm and business just over two years ago, which involved a vast number of legal and financial problems together with the loss of the property we wished to buy. My husband and daughter were both in hospital during that time with serious problems and I was left to deal with everything on my own. It was impossible to find another property that suited us, as we wanted a small amount of land, which was not easy to come by in our price range. In the end we had to settle for something we did not really want and sadly my old mare and donkey were sent to a sanctuary so that they could remain together.

We never really adapted to life without them, but tried to accept the way things were. This changed when our rural existence was abruptly ended. Planning permission was granted for an enormous house to be built right opposite ours and we could stand it no longer. This was the push we must have needed and we sold our house in just over a week, which was strange enough, but even stranger, we spotted the tiniest, most obscure advertisement in our local paper for a property which had only gone on the market the day before. It was in our price range, where we wanted to live and had five beautiful acres and all the outbuildings we could wish for. Better still, we were the first to view the agent's details (which had not yet been printed and the property had not even reached the internet). Our offer was accepted the next day and we were extremely excited. Everything just fell into place and it was as if the other property had only been temporary.

Then the legal process started with all the usual problems buying land involves. Everybody was pushing the solicitors and relationships between the parties were beginning to become tense yet again!

Then the funniest thing happened. A couple of days before Christmas our solicitor telephoned to say a very big thank you for a bottle of whisky received that day at his home. It had a tag with our names on it and he knew of no one else with our names – it had to be us! It definitely was not us, but we had actually considered sending a bottle of whisky on completion of our sale and purchase. How could this have happened?

I am certain that angels intervened somehow, though I've no idea how they brought about the delivery of this gift to keep everything running smoothly for us this time ... Still, I must say it has worked! Our solicitor cannot stop thanking us and insisting that he knows it really was us who sent it!

Maybe you think I'm mad, but I know I'm not. We've just had a wonderful helping hand and everything has worked out fine in the end.

Family Angel

Here is another night-time angel visitor. This one came to see Tracy. She explains:

I was deeply worried at one time about a number of friends and relatives and had a lot of problems sleeping at night. Lots of negative things were happening around me all at the same time and I couldn't understand why so many people were having troubles.

Then one night I was lying in bed fast asleep when something woke me up. I saw a spirit man at the end of my bed. He was dressed in a cream cable-knit jumper and trousers and I just knew he was an angel. He telepathically told me everything was going to be OK and not to worry about my loved ones, as they were being helped from above. I immediately felt happier and went back to sleep.

Even better, everyone's troubles were resolved in a matter of weeks!

Loving Hugs

Sometimes the most amazing things happen for no apparent reason at all. I have included this story here because the phone experience made me laugh. The heavenly message is a strong one, though. Melanie e-mailed over this story:

I woke one night and found myself surrounded by blue light. It was such a vibrant blue and I felt enveloped in so much love that I started crying with the immensity of it. It felt as though the whole universe was wrapping me in love. I didn't want the feeling to go, but the blue light faded and I sat there for a while choked up and crying, so happy to have felt all that love.

This wasn't the first time that someone had written to tell me about a spiritual hug. People usually describe it as the most powerful feeling of love they have ever experienced in their lives. It often comes as the result of great need in their life.

Melanie wasn't sure of any particular reason why she might have experienced this loving feeling at this time, however. But there was more at a time in her life when she *was* struggling:

Another night I woke up and saw an angel looking down on me. He was huge and I only saw his head and shoulders and part of his wings. I felt really comforted and went back to sleep straight away. Perhaps I dreamed it, but even if I did, it brought me the comfort I needed at the time.

There was one more funny incident. When I got home late from work one night and walked through the door my toddler's toy telephone rang, which made me jump out of my skin, as you had to press the numbers to make it ring. Anyway, I stupidly picked the receiver up and said, 'Hello?'

No one was on the other end and I started laughing at myself for answering it. But it could have been my cousin mucking about, letting me know she was still around. It has never rung like that again.

And we already know those angels love to use the telephone!

'We Are with You'

This is another little 'everyday' miracle. Nothing dramatic, but when your greatest need is comfort and reassurance, that can be the biggest miracle in the world.

Steve is from England. He told me:

A couple of years ago I was diagnosed with prostate cancer. I was advised to have a prostectomy operation. I was very nervous and had no confidence that I would live through the operation at all.

Days before my operation I accompanied two of my neighbours to a local Spiritualist church meeting. On this particular night we sang the Abba song 'I Have a Dream' in which the singer says she believes in angels. Immediately I thought to myself, 'If there is such a thing as angels then this is what I could do with next week when I have my operation.'

Thankfully the operation went OK, but I did have to have 19 weeks off work to recuperate. I did wonder if angels had been with me during this time.

I'd been at home a long time and was a little anxious about returning to work. On the first day I drove to work as usual and was listening to my regular radio station. Suddenly the radio switched to another station all on its own – and the song they were playing? 'I Have a Dream'! I was stunned. Tears of happiness were rolling down my face. It seems I hadn't been alone after all.

Mystery and Magic

Now let's examine some of the more mysterious things angels do!

Angels Everywhere

Chuck believes his life has been saved twice by angels and once an angel helped him when he was lost. He explained:

The first incident took place when I was in high school and I was on the way to the dentist's. I hated going and I have to say my mind was elsewhere. I was just about to cross an intersection on foot when I felt a very strong hand grab my arm and jerk me back. When I looked up, a truck was passing by at a pretty good speed. I would have been killed instantly had I stepped into the road. When I turned around there was a tall white-haired man there whose face was as pink as a baby's. It struck me as odd at the time. After I crossed the street I looked round and he was nowhere in sight.

The second incident took place after high-school graduation. I was supposed to meet someone who was giving me a ride to a job on a military base, but I took the wrong route and ended up at the wrong place. I didn't know what to do, so I just waited there. Suddenly the car showed up and I asked the guy how he had found me. He told me he had felt 'something' pulling him that way even though it had been the wrong road!

The last incident took place when I was travelling. I was on a back road and decided to make a U-turn. A young lady was going pretty fast and I saw her as she approached. Her car was headed right for my door when suddenly it struck the front fender of my car instead. When she got out she said she didn't have time to avoid the crash, but 'something' moved her car away from my door and again my life was spared.

Visiting Heaven's Garden

William is from Arizona in the USA. He is a retired college professor and consultant. He received a series of three visions over a decade ago:

For stress relief and relaxation, I would go up into the Arizona mountains to ride my trail bike and walk in the forest. Even through I considered myself atheist/agnostic

> and I was pretty sure that God was in the same category as Santa Claus and the Easter Bunny, I started to look up into the sky on my hands and knees. My requests consisted of asking to be shown the other side. I wanted proof that there was more to my existence than this physical life, because material success had not brought me the peace and happiness that I had hoped for and had worked very hard for in my life.

William prayed for several years when he was alone in the Arizona mountains. Then over a two-week period he had a series of three dreams that he now believes allowed him to see the other side:

> The first two dreams consisted of being shown beauty that was beyond mere words. The forests were a beautiful living green and the lakes were an incredible bluish green that is impossible for me to accurately describe. I floated effortlessly over the scenery about 100 to 200 yards above the ground. In fact, during the second dream it was so beautiful that I went back to where I started, picked someone up in my arms and said, 'You have got to see this.' I carried this person effortlessly so they could share the beauty with me.
>
> I learned many years later that these dreams are referred to as 'garden' or 'Summerland' dreams. They show us the other side of physical existence, what some call 'the astral world' and others call 'heaven'.

> The third dream in this series was so profound and real that there is not a day when I don't think about it. It is so near and dear to me that it feels as though it happened five minutes ago. In this 'vision', I met a woman about 45 years of age with shoulder-length grey hair who was wearing a floor-length grey gown. We were standing about 10 to 15 feet apart and were looking right into each other's eyes. She had a radiant smile that I cannot describe in words. She did not speak to me with a physical voice, as all communication was telepathic.

William's experience with telepathy does mirror many of these dream-type meetings with angels and the other side. Many believe that we are developing or reawakening these telepathic skills as part of our own spiritual growth. With telepathy no lies or deceit of any kind can be passed between souls. We can quite literally 'read' each other's thoughts.

William explained:

> It was instantaneous communication. She had perfect understanding of my past and present feelings, emotions and thoughts. She not only knew what I had done in my life but the reasons why I had done it. She knew about my most selfish acts, even those that I will take to my grave, and yet there was no judgement or condemnation, just perfect acceptance. She understood the hardships in my life and showed me absolute compassion. I could feel acceptance

> and empathy beyond anything I have experienced on Earth.

Like many other stories that people send me, this showed that our lessons as human souls are about sharing love, compassion and understanding for each other rather than gaining merit for our job successes or our payouts to charitable foundations.

William understood:

> It should also be noted that there were no congratulations from this lady in the grey grown for anything good that I had done or for any successes that I had had as a college professor or consultant.
>
> Then I floated towards her and she held out her arms. As we touched we began to vibrate into each other's bodies. This was ecstasy beyond anything I had ever known in my life. Then the dream ended before we completely melted together.
>
> Some people have told me that what I experienced was a spiritual hug. I had never heard of a spiritual hug before or even believed that we survived death.
>
> The thing I remember most about this dream is the total acceptance from this compassionate woman with a sweet smile on her face that knew everything about me.

This sounds very much as though the meeting was with William's spiritual guide or guardian angel. He told me:

My great frustration in telling this story is my immense disappointment in not being able to put into words the beauty of the landscape and the feeling of total acceptance from this lady. I miss her smile and acceptance every day of my life. I sincerely hope that the other side will be that wonderful, because it sure beat anything I have experienced on Earth.

A Strange Warning

Margaret is from Scotland. She told me:

My father has visited me many times since his death. Once he took me flying with angels. It was a magical experience.

Another time I was in bed when my dad came to me and said, 'Your mum needs you,' and he was pointing his finger at me as he said it. Then, raising his voice, he said, 'And I mean *now*.'

I got up the next day and I couldn't get him out of my mind. My mother lived in London and I was in Scotland, so there was a good drive between our locations. But I just knew there was something the matter, so I dialled her number and her partner answered. Well, that was a good clue because normally he never lifted the phone. I asked him, 'Can I speak to my mother please?' He told me right away that she was in the other room and that she was unwell, so he would have to take the phone to her.

When I spoke to her she sounded very faint. I told her she sounded unwell and she agreed. She told me that she had fallen a few days earlier and had been unable to get up. She explained, 'George can't lift me and we are waiting for your brother Gary to pop over, but he hasn't been here for days.'

I was really angry. My mother had just been lying on the floor! I asked her to put George back on the phone. I couldn't help myself and I shouted at him and told him if he didn't phone an ambulance I would get the police onto him for failing to get medical help for my mum.

Afterwards I felt mean because at the time I had no idea he was very ill himself. He didn't even know what to do. I suggested he go and get the neighbour from upstairs. She came on the phone and I explained to her what had happened. Luckily she organized an ambulance to take my mum to hospital. Later the hospital told me how serious her condition had been.

Thank goodness Dad came to warn me about Mum, because I guess she could have been lying on the floor for several more days. Dad was a real angel!

A Watch Is Heaven Sent

Lana is from England. She told me about her fun watch 'coincidence'. Our personal miracles come in all shapes and sizes. Lana explained:

I owned a cheap Timex watch for seven years or so, which I absolutely loved because it looked good and was able to light up in the dark. The strap finally broke on it and I put it in my coat pocket ready to take for repair. I was out cycling with my husband a few days later and the watch disappeared. I was really upset and despite retracing our route, we couldn't find it.

I remembered reading about asking angels for help, so I decided to give it a go. What did I have to lose? I asked my angels to please let me find my watch and my husband slowly drove us round the route again to search. Well, it was a disappointing result and I felt that angels didn't want to know about such a minor issue.

I loved my watch so much that I decided I would simply buy another one just like it, but over the next few days I discovered that type of watch had long since been discontinued. I didn't like the updated version and I couldn't find a watch that suited my requirements anywhere. It was very frustrating.

Then I found myself in a jeweller's shop in Leamington Spa. I described to the lady behind the counter exactly what I was after, but the choice she showed me was limited. I thanked her for her help and literally had my hand on the door handle to leave the shop when the manager came out from the back asking if he could assist. I told him my tale of woe and he guided me to a glass cabinet that had been right beside me and the shop lady, but for some reason we hadn't spotted what was later glaringly obvious. Shocked, I squealed, 'That's my watch!' at rather a high volume, startling other shoppers! Of course it wasn't my actual watch, but one just like it. In fact it had a better-coloured strap than my original, so I was very happy indeed.

As it turned out, had I entered the shop ten minutes later the manager would have been out, because he was due at a funeral.

I shall be keeping a careful eye on this 'heaven-sent' watch now!

Money from an Angel?

On a cold Sunday morning a few days after New Year's Day 2000, Rowena walked up to her local newsagent's to pick up a newspaper to get the year's astrological forecasts. She remembers it was a very cold morning with a light covering of snow on the ground:

I walked around the corner from my flat and noticed something on the ground in the snow: three or four pristine brilliant white feathers! I applied logic and wondered if they could have come out of a rubbish bag, but there was no collection of rubbish at that time of the year, so I walked around to see if anyone had put anything out. Nothing. Was it angels? I wondered whether the feathers could have come from a bird, but in a city all we get is pigeons – 'rats with wings'!

Maybe it was just me, but I thought it was heartening to see objects which were said to symbolize angels at such an auspicious time in the new century.

Then I had another, more poignant experience: a more human-looking angel surprised me in Newcastle city centre. I was withdrawing money from a cashpoint and I thought I had put the money in my purse. I walked away and was already some distance from the cash machine when I was tapped on the shoulder by a man asking me if two £20 notes were mine. I was stunned! Why would a stranger in a city bother to hand over £40? He could easily have slipped the money into his pocket.

Now the most unusual part of all of this was that the man was about my height, but had the brightest blue eyes and most golden-coloured hair I had ever seen! He was so stunning that it looked almost as if he hadn't come from this world. His clothes really stood out too. They were most unusual. He wore a waistcoat of many colours and the rest of his clothes were black. What was so wonderful was that he was smiling and almost pleased and joyful in giving the money to me.

I was simply astounded and took the money and popped it into my purse. Sadly, when I looked up to thank him, he had gone! He'd just disappeared in an instant. I did look for him afterwards, but couldn't find him anywhere.

I am not really sure if I do believe in angels, but there are some very strange things going on in the world!

Drama and Danger

Some angel stories do involve little more than kindness from a stranger. Miracles though they are, it's usually the more dramatic stories we remember the most. These next stories are full of potential danger. Are they examples of angels giving a little helping hand?

Armed Robbers

Sharmaine is from South Africa. She wrote:

> I had an encounter with angels when my mother passed away in 1995. The night she died I was sitting in the passenger seat of the car on my way home. I was very distraught because I'd felt I'd not helped her enough. I closed my eyes and saw a vision of angels taking my mother up in a rainbow to 'the light'. The funny thing was there had been a terrible storm that night and there had been a rainbow outside my mother's hospital window at exactly the time she died.
>
> A few days later I went to bed and was woken up by someone calling my name right in my ear. I got up and went straight to the bedroom window and saw that we were being robbed, so I immediately woke my brother and father up. Thank goodness we scared the robbers away.
>
> Weeks after that we moved to a better area, but even so I was still scared. My father had to go away to Cape Town

for about a week and before he left he told me to walk around the house during the daytime carrying a pellet gun and keeping the dog by my side so that I could make it known that I was armed and protected.

The house had a broken window in the kitchen and I had to stick a piece of cardboard in it as a temporary measure until we could get it fixed. The first night on our own a family friend said he would stay in the garage with all the furniture and I should stay in the house with the dog.

During the night I had a strange dream. I could see my deceased mother standing by the window with her arms stretched out across the gap where the window was broken. She had incredibly bright light around her and was telling four armed men to leave the house because they were not welcome there.

When I woke up the dog was barking and I went to the window to investigate. It was so dark that I couldn't see anything, so I went back to sleep.

The next morning our friend came running around the house shouting wildly for me and when I asked him what was wrong he said that four armed men had come to the house that night and tried to rob us and had fired shots at him. I was stunned! He also said that they had spent a particular amount of time near the kitchen window and he'd spent most of the night in the garage thinking I was dead, so you can imagine his relief when he woke that morning to find me still alive.

I know that my dear mother came to protect me that night and I'm convinced that without her I wouldn't be here today.

Under Fire

Hilary is from Belfast in Northern Ireland and many times during her life she has felt that she has been looked after. Her story is brief but nonetheless dramatic:

I remember one occasion when I was about seven or eight years old and my granny and I were about to board a bus with our family dog for our usual weekend at our caravan. My granddad was finishing work and would follow Granny and me to the caravan park the next day.

Granny and I always took the bus and when we got on that day initially it felt just like the journeys we had made many times before. But then when my granny sat down in her seat the strangest feeling came over me and I found myself telling her not to sit there. I was very insistent and made her get up so the two of us could take our journey on a different part of the bus.

At the time things were bad on the streets – regular fighting was going on, so it was not a safe place to be – but even so, I'd never felt this urge to move seats before. It was a strange feeling.

The journey started off fine but then, as the bus was passing a flashpoint area known as Short Strand, it came under fire from youths throwing bricks, stones and really anything they could get their hands on. We were extremely shaken up by the experience, but luckily unhurt. Sadly, a young man who had taken our previous seat was badly injured and had to be treated in hospital. I always wondered if my guardian angel had intervened that day.

'Power' Shower

When Antonia from England stepped into her shower one day, she had no idea that her morning ritual would be any different from any other – but she was wrong:

My husband and I lived in a bungalow with our two sons, aged three and seven. Early one morning I decided to have a shower as usual. The shower was over the bath and I usually showered and washed my hair before I woke up the boys.

On this particular morning, my three year old woke up a little earlier than normal. I decided I couldn't leave him to play whilst I showered, so instead I just leant over the bath to wash my hair, leaving the bathroom door open so that I could talk to him and hear what he was doing. This was a complete change from my normal routine.

I took the showerhead off its hook to rinse my hair with the water still running, but when I put it back onto the hook, there was a loud bang! A hole was blasted in the copper pipe connected to the shower, and black burn marks covered the wall tiles and the silver flexi-hose attached to the showerhead.

I had no idea what had happened or why it had exploded, but I was left with no electricity, so later in the day I had an electrician come out to inspect the damage. He told me that the shower hadn't been earthed when it had been put in and that I would probably have been killed had I been standing in the shower with the water running over me. Thank goodness my son woke up so early!

Everyone I spoke to afterwards said that my guardian angel must have been watching over me that day and I think so too!

Our angels often appear when we need them most, but just because you don't see, hear or feel them around you, don't ever think for one minute that they're not with you!

CHAPTER 9

Angel Letters

If you woo the company of the angels in your waking hours, they will be sure to come to you in your sleep.

G. D. Prentice

I receive hundreds of letters and e-mails every month through my website and magazine columns. Many of the same questions appear over and over again. I thought it would be fun to share a very small selection of them here, together with my answers.

A Gift from the Angels

Dear Jacky,

I would just like to share a couple of things that angels have had a hand in since I became aware of them.

I had a daughter from my first marriage and later got married again. Although my new husband loved my daughter as his own, he never wanted his own children. This became a strain, to say the least, as I had had overwhelmingly broody feelings for a long time. I would bring the subject up and get shot down in flames many times. Finally I began to ask my angels for help in reaching my husband.

Eventually I persuaded him to try for a baby, assuring him that probably nothing would happen. Anyway, I was walking into the supermarket one Sunday morning and as I got shoulder to shoulder with a woman I didn't know, she suddenly called out, 'It's a girl!' She was calling to someone else in the store, but I immediately took it as a sign for me.

About a month later I bought a pregnancy test and it was positive. Low and behold, I have a beautiful heaven-sent baby girl, who was born on 21 January 2005. She is my little 'angel'.

Kate

Dear Kate,

First of all congratulations on the birth of your daughter. You must be thrilled!

Angels can help us with such things if it is part of our life path, but we do have to be careful not to manipulate the free will of others. Your husband must agree with your plans on some level – as he surely did here on some higher level of consciousness!

The angels in charge of children and childbirth are the Archangels Gabriel, Raphael and Sandalphon. Of course you and your daughter will have your own guardian angels too and can ask for help from any of these at any time.

Jacky

Angels on a Cloud of Perfume?

Hi, Jacky,

I wanted to share an experience with you.

The primary school my two children attend is a three-mile round trip away on foot and as I don't drive, it's a walk I take often. Most of that walk is taken up by a long tree-lined road, which at 2.45 in the afternoon is quite deserted and it is possible to walk the whole length of it without seeing another soul. However, one afternoon in the early January of this year I must have had company!

The walk provides me with an opportunity to think about life in general and about the people that I have lost over the years without any distractions. As bleak January afternoons are not the most uplifting times, my thoughts had wandered in that direction that day and I was feeling quite sad. Towards the end of the walk I found myself saying out loud, 'If there is anyone there, can you please send me a sign?'

Within seconds I found that I had walked into the most amazing smell of what I can best describe as violets. It was incredibly strong. I was so taken aback that for a moment I stood still and looked about me. I have to say I wondered if someone around me was wearing a strong perfume, as there could be no other logical explanation, but there was not a soul to be seen. There were no flowers anywhere either and I was quite a distance from any houses at that particular part of the walk.

The perfume stayed with me for five or six seconds then just as quickly vanished. I was amazed and when I collected my children I told them what had just happened, but when we arrived at the spot on our homeward walk there was no evidence of it at all.

I am positive the angels were lifting my spirits on that bleak afternoon and they certainly did!

Love and peace to you,

Brigitte

Dear Brigitte,

Thank you so much for sharing your lovely story with me. Angels and loved ones on the other side of life do like to bring us scents as a 'gift' of their presence. These gifts can appear at any time, but do often follow occasions when we ask for a sign.

Many people receive psychic scents (clairgustance) when they are 'daydreaming' (ironing, washing up, etc.) and your walk would have created the same type of relaxed state in which you would have been ready to receive a message or sign from your angels!

I am sure this will be the first of many signs that you are always watched over.

Jacky

Which Angel?

Hi, Jacky,

There are so many angels and I forget who does what. I wonder, if I ask angels for help, are my prayers less effective if I don't ask the right angel?

Many thanks,

Gnaeri

Hiya, Gnaeri,

No, it doesn't matter if you forget which angel to ask for something (I usually do, too). Just ask for 'the best possible outcome from the highest possible source' – that will get the job done! – or work with four Archangels: Raphael (healing), Gabriel (communication), Michael (protection) and Ariel (animal and plant life). These cover most problems.

Jacky

'I Want to Be an Angel Expert'

Hey, Jacky,

I feel so confused right now. I've been trying to contact my angels and I've partly succeeded, but now I'm sort of stuck in a position where I don't know what to do. I want to go further in this and become an angel expert, which I know could take a few years. I feel it's part of me and I'm meant to do this.

Please help me out and give me a few ideas on what to do next. I'm only 16, so I can't really travel much to go to workshops, which I would love to do. The closest thing I have to that is a local psychic fayre (around every six to eight weeks).

Hope to hear from you. Thank you so much.

Sarah

Hi, Sarah,

Thank you for writing to me. There is no such thing as an 'expert' really, because we are all learning about these higher realms constantly (yes, even me!) My way of doing things is just one way. There is no right or wrong way and the only rule really is to work with *love*, so do follow your own intuition on the best way for you to work with angels. By all means, though, use as many tips from my books as you feel appropriate for your own path.

Do go to the psychic fayres if you enjoy them because they may help to expand your awareness. Perhaps a friend or relative would accompany you? Don't spend lots of money on having psychic readings, though. Fayres often have workshops which are free or cheap and you can learn so much from those.

Maybe you can save up and buy yourself a pack of angel cards or ask for a pack as a birthday gift (or make your own). Angel cards are safe and it's easy to learn how to use them.

You can find a lot of books in your local library which may help you (you can ask the library to bring in specific titles from other libraries and can also search for titles on the internet). Maybe your friends or family also have books you could borrow. Start to ask around so you don't end up spending a lot of money. My book *An Angel Treasury* (available from the library) has loads of tips on reaching out to your angels.

Just soak it all up, but reject anything that does not feel right to you. Use your own intuition at all times.

Keep a little notebook to record your own experiments and experiences in. (Date your entries.) You can decorate your notebook with pictures of angels (stickers, drawings and so on). Write down your dreams and wishes – and magical experiences.

But remember that there will never come a time when you feel you know *everything*. Life is a journey, not a destination. Just have fun and remember if you want angels to work with you, the most important thing is to ask them.

Jacky

Hello from Mum

Dear Jacky,

I lost my mum in April 2006. We were very close indeed and I was devastated when she left us. Before she went we were discussing her funeral and I asked her to promise me one thing: to please let me know she was settled when she got to heaven.

On the day after her cremation, after dropping some friends off in Manchester my brother and I were driving home when we came to the Atherton turn-off. This is where we are originally from. As we passed it, I heard my mum say to me, 'Hiya, love.' It was as if she was sitting at the side of me, Jacky!

I was given your book *An Angel Saved My Life* at the funeral and thankfully I'm a believer.

Thank you and God bless,

Deryl

Hi, Deryl,

How wonderful that your mother came back to show you she was OK! These experiences are so special.

It also makes me very happy to know that my books are reaching the people who need them. Thank you for your letter.

Jacky

Lots of Questions

Dear Jacky,

I have so many questions, Jacky! I'm absolutely fascinated with this subject, so I hope you don't mind:

How are angels assigned to people?

Do babies and children have 'adult' angels or 'children' who grow up with them?

Do we have the same angels with us throughout our lives or do they change and come and go?

How can I tell if my angel is around?

I feel that I have brilliant spirit guides and angels who really take care of me and I'd like to know what I can do for them to thank them for all of their hard work.

Thank you so much.

With kindest regards,

Kerry

Hi, Kerry,

Thank you for your kind e-mail. Let me see if I can answer all your questions for you.

Guardianship over a soul is agreed before birth. We know who our angels are on a soul level and have agreed to work together before we are born.

Angels are not human souls as such (although we also have spirit guides who are usually human souls who work with us too). They are light beings, so do not have gender or bodies; however, they will often show themselves to us as male or female, child angels or adults. This is for our own comfort. Of course our own loving family of deceased relatives can also be called our 'angels' and they help out from time to time too.

I believe that some angels work with us throughout our lives and others come and go as the need arises (specialist angels with skills and knowledge that we need at particular times in our lives).

There are lots of ways in which you can tell if your angel is around you. You can ask for a little sign – a feeling or a smell (flowers are usual) – or perhaps ask your angels to bring you a white feather.

Thank your angels by being an 'angel' to others. Practise random acts of kindness as often as you can.

Jacky

'Who is My Visitor?'

Dear Jacky,

A couple of nights ago I was lying in bed and I felt somebody sit down on my legs. I was too frightened to look, so I just kept my head turned the other way. Anyway, the next morning I got up and was looking for my son's boots (he hasn't worn them for a long time) and when I found them there was a large white feather sticking out of the top! I think that it's a guardian angel watching over us.

Then the next night the smoke alarm went off at 3.15 a.m. and there was no smoke anywhere (and the alarm is new, so it wasn't the batteries). The following night I was going to bed and the plug on my lamp had been pulled out of the wall. No one had been in the room, so I don't know how this happened.

I'd just like to know if there is a guardian angel looking over me and my son.

Thanks very much.

Ashleen

Dear Ashleen,

In most cases of this type, the 'angels' who are messing around with things in our home are our own loving relatives who are trying to get our attention, usually just to say hello. I love it that you found a feather in your son's boot! Your afterlife loved ones are determined to let you know they are around you for sure.

It is also usual for our loved ones to manipulate electrical and battery-operated objects to get our attention. They can also switch on taps, flicker lights and play your favourite song on the radio!

If you are worried at all, do get an electrician to check things out to be on the safe side, but I don't feel there is anything to worry about here. Next time it happens, just say hello!

Jacky

'Mum and Granddad Are My Angels'

Hi, Jacky,

My mum passed away two months ago and I did not 'feel' her with me at all for a while afterwards.

Then whilst in my garden on Saturday evening I decided to talk to the angels. To my surprise, I felt my granddad come to me and I asked if Mum was with him and it was a 'Yes'! I talked to Granddad and Mum for about five minutes. Her answers came from flickering lights or little noises in the garden.

Mum and Granddad haven't been back since and I don't 'feel' them with me now.

Thanks.

Jonti x

Dear Jonti,

Thank you for your lovely letter. I bet you were thrilled to receive communication from your loved ones. They do long to reassure us that they are safe and well, but don't want us to become dependent on their visits. It is important that we continue with our lives (although many people do continue to receive dream visitations and so on throughout their lives).

It surprises me how many people receive these experiences nowadays – I feel that we have all grown spiritually and the 'veils' between the realms are thinning to allow more and more people to experience these special communications from the other side of life.

By all means do ask your loved ones to pop in from time to time. I am sure they will visit if they can. But it is important to them that your life continues and does not revolve around their visits – that their contact is a wonderful 'occasional extra' in your life. You know that they will always take an interest in your life and I know you will make them proud of you.

Jacky

'Who is My Angel?'

Dear Jacky,

Can you tell me the name of my guardian angel?

Thanks.

Mary

Dear Mary,

Many will disagree with me, but I don't believe our guardian angels have names at all. They work on a vibrational energy and that is their signature. However, as humans we do like to work with a named 'being'. It's much easier for us to communicate if we can work with an identity!

When we ask them, angels will often provide us with a name. Just ask in your head right now and take whatever name comes to you. If you prefer, you can ask for a name to come to you in a dream or a meditation (or use a guided meditation recording – I have produced a *Meet Your Guardian Angel* CD myself which you can buy from many New Age stores or via my website, www.JackyNewcomb.com).

Alternatively, you can just allocate your angel a name – anything you want. Your angel won't mind one bit!

Jacky

I have thoroughly enjoyed compiling this book of very special angel experiences for you.

May your angels always be with you.

Jacky x

Can You Help?

Have you had experiences of your own with angels or mysterious strangers who help and then disappear, psychic children, relatives who reach out from the other side, psychic pets, messages from higher-level beings or light beings about Earth changes or human development, experiences of or visits to the heavenly realms, near-death experiences or contact with beings from other realms or dimensions, contact with nature spirits (faeries) or warnings or information from other dimensions which helped you or saved your life? If so, I would love to hear from you! Drop me an e-mail at my website: **www.JackyNewcomb.com**

Thank you!

About the Author

Jacky Newcomb is one of the UK's leading paranormal writers and angel experts. She has a great interest in angels, spirit guides, psychic children, afterlife communication and all things mystical and paranormal. Jacky has had many paranormal and angel experiences during her own lifetime, many of which she has written about in her books. She has studied a wide range of paranormal and psychic phenomena and holds a diploma in psychic development. Jacky is also a Reiki Master.

Jacky is the author of the hugely popular *An Angel Saved My Life*, her first collection of stories of the afterlife, as well as *An Angel Treasury*, *A Little Angel Love* and *An Angel by My Side*. Her work has featured in the UK's foremost paranormal and mystical magazines including *Chat – It's Fate*, *Fate & Fortune*, *Prediction* and *Vision*. In addition she has produced features and articles for many non-paranormal women's magazines in the UK and around the world including *CHAT*, *My Weekly* and *Woman's Own*.

She runs several mystical 'agony aunt' columns and receives hundreds of queries and questions about paranormal experiences on her website and in response to her magazine and newspaper columns.

Jacky has acted as a consultant on several paranormal shows and magazine features, and been interviewed on television programmes such as ITV's *This Morning*, the Lorraine Kelly Show *LK Today* and LIVINGtv's *Psychic Live*. She is regularly interviewed on radio about her work.

Jacky is one of the presenters on the DVD *Angels* (for New World Music), and has recorded several guided meditations for Paradise Music. Signed copies of Jacky's books and other products are available at:

www.JackyNewcomb.com

Jacky lives with her husband John and her two daughters in a small Staffordshire village, along with their cats Tigger and Magik.

For more information about Jacky and her work, visit her website, or write to her via HarperCollins*Publishers* (77–85 Fulham Palace Road, Hammersmith, London W6 8JB), remembering to enclose a stamped addressed envelope if you want a personal reply. Or, to ensure a reply, try e-mail, which is much quicker (jackytheangel-lady@yahoo.com)!